The Quantified Self

The Quantified Self

A Sociology of Self-Tracking

Deborah Lupton

polity

First published in 2016 by Polity Press

Polity Press
65 Bridge Street
Cambridge CB2 1UR, UK

Polity Press
350 Main Street
Malden, MA 02148, USA

ISBN-13: 978–1–5095–0059–8
ISBN-13: 978–1–5095–0060–4(pb)

A catalogue record for this book is available from the British Library.

Library of Congress Cataloging-in-Publication Data

Names: Lupton, Deborah.
Title: The quantified self / Deborah Lupton.
Description: Malden, MA : Polity, 2016. | Includes bibliographical references and index.
Identifiers: LCCN 2015034998| ISBN 9781509500598 (hardcover : alk. paper) | ISBN 1509500596 (hardcover : alk. paper) | ISBN 9781509500604 (pbk. : alk. paper) | ISBN 150950060X (pbk. : alk. paper)
Subjects: LCSH: Self-actualization (Psychology) | Reflection (Philosophy) | Digital media–Social aspects.
Classification: LCC BF637.S4 L85 2016 | DDC 158.1–dc23 LC record available at http://lccn.loc.gov/2015034998

Typeset in 10.5 on 12 pt Sabon
by Toppan Best-set Premedia Limited
Printed and bound in the UK by CPI Group (UK) Ltd, Croydon

For further information on Polity, visit our website: politybooks.com

For Gamini Colless, my favourite self-tracker

Contents

Acknowledgements

This book draws and expands on the material I have presented in several posts on my blog, 'This Sociological Life' (http://simplysociology.wordpress.com), as well as on four previously published academic articles:

Lupton, D. (2012) M-health and health promotion: The digital cyborg and surveillance society. *Social Theory and Health*, 10 (3): 229–44.

Lupton, D. (2013) Quantifying the body: Monitoring and measuring health in the age of mHealth technologies. *Critical Public Health*, 23 (4): 393–403.

Lupton, D. (2013) Understanding the human machine. *IEEE Technology & Society Magazine*, 32 (4): 25–30.

Lupton, D. (2014) Self-tracking cultures: Towards a sociology of personal informatics. In *Proceedings of the Twenty-sixth Australian Computer–Human Interaction Conference on Designing Futures 'The Future of Design'*, 77–86. Sydney, Australia: ACM (Association for Computing Machinery).

I thank the two anonymous reviewers of the draft manuscript of this book for their helpful and constructive comments and suggestions.

Introduction

The concept of self-tracking using digital technologies has recently begun to emerge in discussions of the ways in which people can conduct their lives. Monitoring, measuring and recording elements of one's body and life as a form of self-improvement or self-reflection are practices that have been discussed since ancient times. The introduction of digital technologies that facilitate these practices has led to renewed interest in what self-tracking can offer and to an expansion of the domains and purposes to which these practices are applied.

This book is about contemporary self-tracking cultures, analysed from a critical sociological perspective. I use the term 'cultures' to encapsulate the view, adopted throughout the book, that the practices, meanings, discourses and technologies associated with self-tracking are inherently and inevitably the product of broader social, cultural and political processes. The book examines the influences, discourses, technologies, power relations and systems of thought that contribute to the phenomenon of self-tracking, the ways in which this phenomenon is spreading from the private realm into diverse social domains, and the implications of the self-tracking phenomenon for the politics of personal data, data practices and data materialisations.

Self-tracking practices are directed at regularly monitoring and recording, and often measuring, elements of an individual's behaviours or bodily functions. Some self-trackers simply collect information about themselves as a way of remembering and recording aspects of their lives, or to satisfy their curiosity about the patterns in their behaviours or body metrics that they may uncover. Others take an approach that is more specifically goal-oriented, seeking as they do to reflect on and make meaning out of the information they choose to collect and to discern patterns that will work to improve features such as their health, physical fitness, emotional well-being, social relationships or work productivity. Some self-trackers collect data on only one or two dimensions of their lives, and only for a short time. Others may do so for hundreds of phenomena and for long periods.

My interpretation of self-tracking in this book rests on the assumption that it involves practices in which people knowingly and purposively collect information about themselves, which they then review and consider applying to the conduct of their lives. Self-tracking differs, therefore, from covert surveillance or means of collecting information on people that result in data sets to which the subjects of monitoring do not have access. As I go on to demonstrate in later chapters, many forms of personal information are generated by people's routine engagements and transactions online or by their movements in spaces that are embedded with sensors or fitted with cameras that monitor them. Only a small proportion of this information is accessible to the subjects of this monitoring. Indeed in many cases people have no knowledge of what data are collected on them, where these data are stored and to what purposes they are used by other actors and agencies. These are examples not of self-tracking, but of tracking of the self by others.

Several terms in addition to self-tracking are used to describe the practices by which people may seek to monitor their everyday lives, bodies and behaviours; such terms are lifelogging, personal informatics, personal analytics and the quantified self. Lifelogging tends to be used to refer to the specific practice of using wearable computing devices such as cameras, sensors, and other computerised and automated ways of collecting personal information over a period of time.

The practice is not necessarily about self-improvement but may also be undertaken as a form of computerised memory or as a kind of recording information about a person's life for future generations. Personal informatics and personal analytics are terms that are used most often in academic literature on human–computer interaction. The title of this book denotes 'the 'quantified self' – a new term for describing self-monitoring practices that was invented in 2007 and has since gathered cultural resonance. While the quantified self overtly refers to using numbers as a means of monitoring and measuring elements of everyday life and embodiment, it can be interpreted more broadly as an ethos and apparatus of practices that has gathered momentum in this era of mobile and wearable digital devices and of increasingly sensor-saturated physical environments.

I first became interested in contemporary self-tracking cultures when I came across a reference to the Quantified Self movement in a news story a few years ago. I had a look at the Quantified Self website (Quantified Self, 2015c) and was fascinated to see the types of practices that 'quantifying the self' and attempting 'self-knowledge through numbers' (the site's motto) involved. As an academic in the fields of sociology and media and cultural studies who has written on a range of related topics (such as embodiment, selfhood, health and medicine, risk and digital cultures), I am interested in analysing self-tracking as a sociocultural phenomenon. My initial response to self-tracking was that it was an intriguing way of using forms of information to conduct practices of selfhood and embodiment. This, in itself, is an interesting topic to explore. However, over the period in which I have observed and sought to analyse self-tracking, it has become clear that the practice has expanded well beyond the domain of the individual, into a variety of social contexts and uses. In many cases self-tracking is a purely voluntary personal enterprise initiated by the person who is engaging in it. However, there are various ways in which self-tracking is being encouraged, or even enforced on people, predominantly so that the objectives of others are met; and such ways raise the question of exactly how voluntary self-tracking may be in these contexts. People are now frequently encouraged, 'nudged', obliged or coerced into monitoring aspects of their lives so as to produce personal data that can then also be used for the purposes of others.

The digitisation of self-tracking has been a major impetus in these changes. Writing down thoughts in diaries or journals and recording everyday habits or body measurements through the time-honoured technologies of pen and paper are avenues of self-monitoring that have long-established histories. They remain practices in which some self-trackers continue to engage. Since the advent of computing, however, self-tracking has been transformed into major interconnected practices that have significant social, cultural and political implications.

First, the technologies and practices of self-tracking have become progressively digitised and automated, facilitating the ever more detailed measurement and monitoring of the body and everyday life in real time. Accessing information generated through digital technologies and sharing it with others are greatly facilitated via the processes of searching, retrieval and tagging with the help of software. Second, these personal details are now typically transmitted to and stored on cloud computing databases. As a consequence, accessibility to these details is no longer limited to the self-trackers themselves, as was the case in the days of paper journals and records, but personal details are potentially available to other actors and agencies. These include the developers of the devices and software that self-trackers use; third parties that may purchase these data from such developers; data-mining companies and their clients; and government agencies. Cybercriminals or hackers may illegally access the data and steal them for profit or malicious purposes. This has major repercussions on the privacy and security of the details that self-trackers collect about their bodies and lives, which are often of a very sensitive and intimate nature. And, finally, this personal information has become endowed with significant commercial and managerial value, as part of the digital data knowledge economy.

I employ the concept of 'lively data' in this book and frequently return to this concept in my efforts to theorise self-tracking cultures. I first came across this description of digital data in an article by Mike Savage (2013) in which the author used the phrase 'lively data' to denote the constant generation of large masses of digital data as part of the digital data economy, and the implications of this practice for sociological research methods. Dave Beer's (2013) and Dave Beer and Roger Burrows' (2013) work on the circulations and politics of digital data has also contributed to my thinking about the vitality of these knowledge forms.

In my own work I have developed the notion of lively data still further, so as to denote the manifold ways in which personal digital data (whether deliberately generated for individuals' own purposes or collected by others about them) are vital. Not only are personal digital data continually generated, as Savage emphasises, but they are fundamentally about the lives of humans: about their bodily functions, behaviours, social relationships, moods and emotions. Digital data generate new forms of knowledge and new insights into people's bodies and selves. They are also contributing to livelihoods by generating profit for those who use them commercially or by facilitating the management and governance of people and populations. Furthermore, as outlined by Beer and Burrows (2013), these data have a vitality of their own in the digital data economy by virtue of the fact that they circulate, enact new forms of knowledge and are purposed and repurposed in many different ways. In other words they have their own social lives, which are quite independent of the humans who originally generated them. Digital data about people's lives are also vital in their effects. As I explain in greater detail later in this book, they have begun to play a significant role in influencing people's behaviours, sense of self, social relationships and, increasingly, their life chances and opportunities. Digital data have implications for people's employment, research material and profit. All of these properties of digital data are important to consider in a sociological analysis of self-tracking.

From a sociological perspective, a number of interesting questions arise about the quest for monitoring and measuring elements of one's body, behaviour and habits. What are the tacit assumptions that underpin contemporary modes of self-tracking? Why are people attracted to self-tracking? How do they interpret and use the data they produce? How are concepts of the body, self, social relationships and social behaviours configured and negotiated via these data? How have the ethos and practices of self-tracking been appropriated by other actors and agencies? What implications are there for data politics, data practices and the digital data knowledge economy? What are the power relations and power inequalities inherent in self-tracking cultures?

The book discusses all of these issues. In making my arguments I draw on material from a range of sources such as app and software descriptions and product reviews, news reports, white papers, social media and blog discussions – in addition to the existing literature on self-tracking published by researchers in the social sciences and human–computer interaction studies. To keep up to date with discussions on self-tracking, I used tools such as Twitter hashtags (#quantifiedself, #lifelogging and #selftracking), the Quantified Self website and various other websites devoted to self-tracking for regularly checking the content that people posted. A weekly update of articles and blog posts about self-tracking, collated by the Quantified Self website organisers, has been an invaluable resource. I searched for the work of artists and designers who are engaging in self-tracking practices (I viewed some exhibitions in person); and I checked for news reports on self-tracking by searching the web and by using the news database Factiva.

In Chapter 1, after a discussion of the early lifeloggers and experimental attempts to use wearable computing devices for self-tracking, I provide an overview of the varieties of self-tracking devices, apps and other software that are currently available. The chapter ends with a review of market research and academic studies that have sought to identify what types of people engage in self-tracking and how and why they do so. Chapter 2 reviews ways of analysing self-tracking rationales and practices from various sociocultural theoretical perspectives. These approaches offer opportunities to delve below the surface meanings and rationales of self-tracking cultures and to illuminate how these cultures operate and what the wider implications of their practices are. The discussion begins by outlining the value of sociomaterial perspectives and continues with more specific reviews of knowing capitalism and lively data, practices of selfhood and neoliberal politics, the cultural dimensions of embodiment, datafication, dataveillance and privacy.

The following three chapters then go on to build on these two initial overview chapters by concentrating closely on elements of self-tracking cultures. Chapter 3 focuses on portrayals and representations of the body and the self in self-tracking cultures, incorporating analysis of the reflexive monitoring self, affective dimensions of self-tracking, concepts of embodiment and control, and selfhood and surveillance. In Chapter 4 I move on to analysing the ways in which data are discussed and conceptualised as part of self-tracking. I examine the meaning and value of personal digital data; metricisation and the lure of numbers; materialisations of the data; artistic and design responses; and qualified selves and the importance of context. In the final substantive chapter, Chapter 5, I address the important issue of data politics. The chapter outlines in detail the ways in which the personal information generated through self-tracking is used by second and third parties. The discussion covers the modes of exploited, pushed, imposed and communal self-tracking, personal data security and privacy, and strategies of resistance to dataveillance. In the brief 'Final Reflections' chapter that concludes the book, I summarise its major themes and make some suggestions concerning the ways in which self-tracking cultures and practices, as well as academic research on these phenomena, might further develop.

1

'Know Thyself'

Self-Tracking Technologies and Practices

The tracking and analysis of aspects of one's self and one's body are not new practices. People have been recording their habits and health-related metrics for millennia, as part of attempts at self-reflection and self-improvement. What is indisputably new is the term 'the quantified self' and its associated movement, as well as the novel ways of self-tracking with the help of digital technologies that have developed in recent years. In this chapter I discuss contemporary self-tracking practices and technologies, from the days of early lifelogging techniques and wearable computing devices with which people experimented in the 1990s to the vast array of technologies that are available today. This is followed by a review of existing empirical research, which has focused on those who take up self-tracking and their experiences.

The emergence of contemporary self-tracking

As I noted in the Introduction, various terms have been used over the years to describe self-tracking practices: lifelogging, personal informatics, personal analytics and the quantified self. Lifelogging is the most established term. The practice of lifelogging, under this name, emerged in the early days of personal computing, as computing engineers in research labs were experimenting with techniques and technologies (Sellen and Whittaker, 2010). Gordon Bell, an American computer scientist at Microsoft Research, is well known for his long-term lifelogging project. Bell took inspiration from an idea expounded by the American presidential science advisor, Vannevar Bush, who wrote an essay published in 1945 in which he asserted his belief that humans' ability to remember could be enhanced by technology. In this essay Bush introduced his idea of the Memex, a mechanised device in which people could store all their documents, records, books, letters and memos, as well as newspapers and an encyclopaedia. He suggested that people could also wear small cameras on their foreheads to capture details of their daily lives and add them to the Memex archive (MyLifeBits, 2015; Thompson, 2006). Beginning in 1998, Gordon Bell attempted to record as many aspects of his life as possible using digital technologies, including all his correspondence and documents (scanning paper documents as well as storing emails and so on), books he had read, photos, home movies and videos, computer files, mementos, meetings, conversations and phone calls. Bell started wearing a camera in 2000 and an early health-tracking armband, BodyMedia, in 2002. He instigated the MyLifeBits project for Microsoft, expanding on this endeavour (MyLifeBits, 2015).

The developers of wearable computing devices were also among the earliest to experiment with monitoring aspects of their lives through these technologies. The first international symposium on wearable computers was held in 1997 and included papers that focused mainly on the uses of such devices (for example head-mounted devices and clothing embedded with sensors) for performing work-related tasks (IEEE, 1997). The symposium also discussed using wearable technologies for the performing arts, identifying emotions in the wearer, assisting people with disabilities, and telemedicine.

The Canadian computing engineer Steve Mann, a contributor to this first symposium, was one of the most prominent advocates of and experimenters with wearable computers in those early days. Mann began experimenting with using wearable computers in the 1970s. By the early 1980s he was using these devices, which to contemporary eyes appear very chunky and clunky, for recording personal information about his daily activities. Mann founded the MIT Wearable Computing Project at the MIT Media Lab in 1992. From 1993 on he wore a webcam and recorded and broadcast details of his everyday life in a continuous live feed, as part of his Wearable Wireless Webcam project. By 1998 Mann had reduced the size of his wearable recording device considerably and was wearing a pendant containing a camera as part of his attempts to create what he called a 'lifeglog' (a shortened version of the term 'cyborglog' or computerised automated lifelog) (Mann, 1997, 2013).

Artists and designers have experimented with lifelogging and wearable technologies for several decades. In 1974 Andy Warhol began a 'time capsule' project that continued until his death in 1987. It involved placing items that crossed his desk into cardboard boxes: books, catalogues, letters, photographs, newspapers and magazines, invitations and so on. By the time he died, he had accumulated over six hundred filled boxes, the contents of which have become archived and preserved at the Andy Warhol Museum (Allen, 2008). On Kawara, a Japanese conceptual artist who lived most of his adult life in the United States, spent decades noting down details of the people he met each day, the places he visited and the books he read. He developed a massive archive of these details that he enshrined in bound volumes. During an 11-year period, Kawara sent a postcard each day to friends and colleagues, recording the time he had awoken that morning and his geographical location. Each day for almost half a century – from 1966 to 2013 – Kawara also produced a 'date painting' recording each day's date; the 'date painting' was often accompanied by a storage box that usually contained a cutting from a newspaper published on that date. Another conceptual artist, the Italian Alberto Frigo, has embarked on a long-term lifelogging project that began when he was 24 and has spanned more than a decade thus far (Frigo, 2015). He plans to continue until 2040, when he turns 60: hence the title of his project, '2004–2040'. The project involves photographing every object that his right hand uses, as a way of monitoring his everyday activities. Frigo has also begun recording many other aspects of his life: details of his dreams, the songs he listens to, the external surroundings in which he moves each day, people he meets, new ideas, cloud shapes and the daily weather.

Developments in small-scale computerised technologies in the 1990s inspired many designers to experiment with wearable fashion and other objects that could be worn on the body, such as jewellery. Several of these designs involved methods of tracking and displaying elements of the wearers' bodies. An area of human–computing research also developed in this era, called 'affective computing' or 'affective wearables', which concentrated on working on wearables that were embedded with sensors designed to read users' emotional states and communicate them to others (Picard, 2000). The design arms of companies such as the electronics company Philips developed such prototypes. In 2008, for instance, Philips released a prototype called Fractals, digital jewellery or scarf arrangements that were designed to be a hybrid between clothing and jewellery. These objects sensed bodily changes of the wearer as well as the proximity of others' bodies, using LED (light-emitting diode) configurations to display the data that they gathered (Ryan, 2014).

Perhaps the most public face of self-tracking these days is the Quantified Self website. The term 'quantified self' was invented in 2007 by two *Wired* magazine editors, Gary Wolf and Kevin Kelly. They went on to establish meeting groups for interested people and then set up the official website (see Quantified Self, 2015c) and its associated Quantified Self Labs – a collaboration of users and toolmakers who are interested in working together to share technical expertise and experiences of self-tracking. The Quantified Self website provides discussion forums, supports regional meetings of members and two annual international conferences (QS Global in California and QS Europe in Amsterdam), and publishes a blog in which various aspects of self-tracking are explained and the strategies and findings of members about their own self-tracking efforts are publicised. An academic research institute, named the Quantified Self Institute, has also been established in the Netherlands by the Hanze University of Applied Science in collaboration with the Quantified Self Labs. According to the Quantified Self website, as of July 2015 there were 207 quantified self 'meetup' groups in 37 countries around the world, with a total of over 52,000 members (Quantified self meetup groups, 2015). Many of these groups hold regular meetings involving 'show-and-tell' discussions of how members have been engaging in self-tracking activities. Most of the groups are in the United States, but there are also many in Europe, ten in Asia and two in Australia.

As a journalist specialising in digital technologies and as co-founder of the Quantified Self movement, Gary Wolf has played a major role in announcing the quantified-self ethos and outlining its development. He wrote an initial article seeking to explain the concept of the quantified self for *Wired*. It was entitled 'Know thyself: Tracking every facet of life, from sleep to mood to pain, 24/7/365' (Wolf, 2009). Wolf's first paragraph described some of the numbers he has collected on his own life. These included the time he rose from bed each morning, how often he woke during the night, his heart rate, blood pressure, the time he spent exercising in the past 24 hours, his caffeine and alcohol consumption and his narcissism score. He went on to claim that '[n]umbers are making their way into the smallest crevices of our lives' due to the digital devices that can now collect detailed, continuous data on everyday practices, social interactions and bodily functions (ibid.).

Later in this article Wolf described the genesis of the Quantified Self movement. He recounted how, two years earlier, he and Kelly had begun to notice that many acquaintances of theirs were gathering quantitative data about themselves: 'A new culture of personal data was taking shape. The immediate cause of this trend was obvious: New tools had made self-tracking easier' (ibid.). Wolf wrote that he and Kelly then decided to establish a website bearing the title 'Quantified Self', a term that they had come up with to describe this phenomenon of detailed digitised self-tracking. Wolf went on to give a TED (Technology, Entertainment and Design) talk about the quantified self in 2010 and wrote an article on the topic for *The New York Times* that same year (Wolf, 2010).

Since the initial *Wired* article penned by Wolf, the Quantified Self as a subculture has exerted increasing influence over the definition and practices of self-tracking. The term 'quantified self' has now entered the cultural lexicon. My research suggests that its frequency of use has been increasing and gathering momentum annually. In July 2015 I made a Google Trends graph comparing the terms 'self-tracking', 'lifelogging', and 'quantified self' to see relatively how often each has been used in Google searches: this was an indicator (if only a crude one) of online searchers' interest in each term. (Google Trends is an open tool that shows how often a particular search term has been entered into Google Search by comparison to other searches globally.) The graph showed that it was not until late 2007 that 'self-tracking' and 'lifelogging' began to be recognised. The term 'quantified self' only began to appear in the graph in May 2010 (not surprisingly, given that it was first coined in 2007) but rose quickly in popularity, beginning to overtake 'self-tracking' by January 2012. The volume of searches for 'self-tracking' and 'quantified self' began to converge in mid-2014, although results for 'quantified self' have remained higher for most months. 'Lifelogging' began to lose currency by early 2010 and has remained steady, but much lower in relative volume than the other terms ever since.

Interest in the quantified self among Google searchers was no doubt encouraged by news media interest, which has also grown steadily since 2009. The term has spread from being a proper noun that referred specifically to the official Quantified Self website and community to being now used as a common noun – a general term for self-tracking practices. Descriptions such as 'the quantified organisation', 'the quantified patient', 'the quantified doctor', 'the quantified body', 'quantified sex', 'the quantified home', 'the quantified mind', 'the quantified baby', and even 'the quantified pet' have appeared in popular cultural artefacts such as blog posts and news items, demonstrating the taking up of the term 'quantified self' and its application to more specific topics.

A study of reporting of the quantified self that I conducted using the Factiva global newspaper database to search for English-language articles that mentioned this term in the six years period between January 2009 and July 2015 found that it was increasingly prevalent in news articles over this period. In 2009 only two news articles appeared mentioning the quantified self: one, in the American *Life Science Weekly*, reported a study on the relevance of self-tracking to healthcare; and the other, in the Canadian *Globe and Mail*, discussed the Quantified Self movement and the people involved in it. However, the number of articles rose to 21 in 2010 and 33 in 2011, and by 2012 148 articles had been published that used the term. The year 2013 witnessed greater interest: by the end of that year 466 news articles discussing the quantified self had been published. This figure rose even higher in 2014, when 564 articles appeared.

My review of the news media coverage of the quantified self found that the tenor and scope of reporting the phenomenon have also changed since the initial publication of news stories. Early news reports focused on the innovative aspects of quantifying the self and debated whether such close attention to the details of a person's life and bodily functions would extend beyond 'uber geeks' – those 'weirdly narcissistic' few who are interested in 'extreme naval gazing' to the general population, as *Forbes* magazine put it (25 April 2011). By 2012 news articles represented quantified-self practices as growing in popularity and becoming not only an important feature of health promotion but a part of everyday life, as a way of maximising productivity and happiness as well as health. As the British *Sunday Telegraph Magazine* (2 December 2012) contended: 'It began with a small group of digital obsessives recording their every heartbeat. Today the "quantified self" movement is a gadget-filled fitness craze.' By June 2013, *The Guardian* (UK) was asserting that 'the "Quantified Self" movement [is] all the rage for people tracking their physical activity, food intake, vital signs and even their personal genome through digital services'.

Data privacy and security issues concerning the personal information that is generated by self-tracking devices began to receive attention in the later years of reporting. A *Forbes* magazine report (31 July 2014), for example, referred to a new market research report that found that there were numerous data security risks associated with a large number of self-tracking apps and devices that were examined. This meant that the personal data uploaded to these technologies could easily be accessed by others and on-sold to third parties for commercial gain. Several articles raised the question of whether people were becoming too obsessed with digital self-tracking and focusing on their numbers to the exclusion of other aspects of their lives. *The Guardian* (7 March 2015) published an account by a woman who believed that she had fallen into this trap to the point where she had asked herself: 'Do I even exist without my Fitbit? Without data, am I dead?' Reference was made, in a *Toronto Star* news story of 19 January 2015, to the 'big data junkies' who 'self-hack' incessantly. Despite these concerns, news articles have continued to report on the apparent popularity of wearable devices for self-tracking and on the opportunities for developers to profit from them. An Australian *Business Insider* report, for example, claimed that, '[in] just a few years, there could be more people using wearable tech devices than there are in the US and Canada' (15 July 2015).

Contemporary self-tracking technologies

Digitised self-tracking has attracted a high level of attention from developers and entrepreneurs seeking to capitalise on the practice. They are taking a keen interest in how best to produce technologies to market to self-trackers, and often attend quantified-self meetups and conferences (Boesel, 2013; Nafus and Sherman, 2014). The range and variety of self-tracking technologies that are now available, particularly new digital devices and software, are vast. The Quantified Self website lists over 500 self-tracking tools; in addition to geo-location, these include health-, fitness-, weight-, sleep-, diet- and mood- or emotion-tracking apps, services and devices that are able to record social interactions, emails, networks and social media status updates and comments (Quantified Self, 2015b). Other tools noted there allow users to track their meditation practices, television watching, computer use and driving habits, financial expenses, time use, beneficial habits and work productivity, and to monitor local environmental conditions, progress towards learning or the achievement of personal goals (see also the Personal Informatics website for another long list of tools: Personal Informatics, 2015).

The use of sensors is a pivotal feature of contemporary self-tracking technologies. Many different types of digital sensors are now used to monitor a diverse array of aspects of human and nonhuman activity. Biosensor devices collect data from living organisms or systems. They contribute to self-tracking efforts to monitor bodily phenomena or elements of the physical environment. Biosensors include reactive agents that can respond to changes in bodily functions and indicators – such as blood glucose, hormone, enzyme or oxygen levels. Once used only by healthcare workers, environmental scientists or people with chronic illnesses who engage in self-management of their condition, biosensors are now available far more widely to the general public. Indeed smartphones now routinely include sensors such as global positioning systems (GPS), digital compasses, gyroscopes and accelerometers that can be employed for monitoring people's movements and geolocation. Some smartphones incorporate heart rate, body temperature, humidity, atmospheric pressure and air temperature sensors.

Tens of thousands of self-tracking apps are available for downloading to smartphones and iPod devices that can draw on the information collected by built-in sensors on the device or facilitate the input of other data by the user on his or her everyday activities and behaviours. Some technologies offer a genetic component to self-tracking, as individuals seek to identify their genomic profile, including their racial ancestry and risk of developing certain diseases and conditions. Various internet-based companies now offer services for members of the public to send in DNA (desoxyribonucleic acid) samples and have their genotypes identified (this is often referred to as direct-to-consumer personal genomics). Some such companies, for example 23andMe, are establishing large digital databases containing the genetic information of their customers.

Many devices equipped with sensors and other forms of digital tracking are now wearable. The wireless wearable heart-rate monitor was one of the first technologies to move out of the clinic and into the domain of fitness and exercise tracking (Pantzar and Ruckenstein, 2015). There is a now growing number of specifically designed wearable devices such as the Fitbit, Jawbone's Up and Nike Fuelband, which can be worn as bracelets or clipped onto belts. Various brands of adhesive patches are available for self-tracking, as are ingestible digital tablets that send wireless signals from inside the body to a patch worn on the arm. All of these are designed to automatically collect data on bodily functions such as physical activity, pulse, breathing rate, heart rate, body temperature, calories burned, brain waves and sleep patterns. Some can be worn 24 hours a day, in order to provide constant readings of biometrics. Attachments to smartphones can be purchased that effectively turn them into medical devices – enabling pregnant women to monitor their foetus' heart rate, for example. Digital body weight scales, ECG (electrocardiogram) devices for measuring heart function, blood oxygen saturation monitors and blood-pressure monitors that link to smartphones are also on the market for the lay consumer.

Telehealth and telemedicine technologies have been in existence since the 1990s, involving computerised devices located within patients' homes to facilitate remote monitoring of their bodies. Digitised wireless patient self-care and self-monitoring devices are an important element of the latest array of self-tracking technologies. Such technologies as continuous glucose monitoring are now available for controlling diabetes via a device that is inserted within the patient's body, checks blood glucose in the surrounding tissues constantly and sends the information wirelessly to an external unit. Self-tracking devices are currently expanding into a greater number of medical and health applications. Arguments for persuading patients with chronic illnesses to engage in self-tracking through the latest wireless devices are becoming increasingly common in the medical literature. The British National Health Service (NHS) is working on rolling out such devices as part of preventive medicine and patient self-care. The Obama Administration's Affordable Care Act has similarly championed at-home medical self-monitoring devices as part of its initiative to reduce healthcare costs by decreasing the number of patient admissions to hospital. The American National Institutes of Health (NIH) is investigating ways of encouraging citizens to engage in voluntary digital self-tracking designed to generate big data sets for research as part of the Precision Medicine Initiative.

In health education and health promotion there is a long tradition of encouraging members of the public to take note of such aspects as their body weight or abdominal measurements, physical activity, diet and alcohol or cigarette consumption as part of improving their health status (Lupton, 1995b). These attempts to change target groups' behaviours are now incorporating the use of digital devices. Health promoters and health educators are using an expanding array of self-tracking devices as part of their preventive health efforts; such devices include encouraging people to use health- and fitness-monitoring technologies and apps. Health-promotion organisations and agencies have developed apps and platforms of their own, custom-designed for such purposes, or else they advocate the use of health and fitness self-tracking apps and devices that are commercially available. These are represented as behavioural interventions designed to encourage adherence to health-promoting objectives (Lupton, 2012, 2015b).

The internet empires are now entering the wearable self-tracking technology arena. Amazon has opened a specialist wearable technology store on its website. In 2014 Apple, Samsung and Google all announced new wearable devices that have self-tracking functions. Apple released its smartwatch, the Apple Watch, in April 2015. Among its other functions, the Apple Watch acts as a wearable health- and fitness-tracking device. Apart from allowing customers to use third-party apps, it incorporates two new apps, simply called 'Fitness' and 'Workout', which operate with its embedded sensors to track users' physical activities and heart rate. According to Tim Cook, Apple's CEO (chief executive officer), the Watch is viewed by Apple as 'the most personal device we've ever created' – both because it is worn on the body, potentially 24 hours a day, and because it can act as a 'personal trainer' (Colt, 2014). Apple has also moved into the realm of facilitating the collection and use of personal data for medical research. It has partnered with several medical research institutions to enrol people into health research projects that use apps on Apple mobile devices that collect users' health, medical and fitness information as part of its Research-Kit software platform. Samsung has developed the Galaxy smartphone and Galaxy Gear smartwatch, both of which are endowed with biometric monitoring capabilities. In 2014 Google announced its Google Fit platform, which is directed at allowing health- and fitness-tracking apps from different developers to access data across platforms.

The range of wearable fashion objects that track the wearer's bodily functions through sensor-embedded smart fabrics is expanding into the production of clothing, hats, helmets and shoes. Gloves, arm bands and devices meant to be placed on sporting equipment are on sale that can monitor sporting activities such as golfing, tennis or baseball swings, while sensor-embedded basketballs and footballs track sporting prowess. Face-worn devices and cameras that can be mounted on sporting equipment are also available that can be used to record and capture images and geolocation data or be integrated with sport- and fitness-tracking apps and platforms. Some fashion designers are working on high-fashion clothing and jewellery that are able both to collect information on the wearer and to look appealing. One example is the collaboration of the jewellery company Swarovski with Misfit in developing crystal-encrusted fitness and sleep trackers. High-end fashion-design house Ralph Lauren has developed a 'Polo Tech Shirt' embedded with body metric sensors, while several companies have developed stylish headphones or earbuds that pipe music into users' ears while simultaneously measuring their heart rate.

In a far less glamorous context, self-tracking is used in programs that involve monitoring location and drug use for probation and parole surveillance, alcohol and drug addiction programs, and family law and child custody monitoring. Digital cellular monitoring devices allow the radio frequency monitoring of offenders who are serving at-home sentences. In some criminal justice systems global positioning technologies are also used to track parolees' movements. Several self-tracking devices for monitoring alcohol use have been developed for use in programs for alcohol addiction and policing. The secure continuous remote alcohol-monitoring device is used to provide alcohol testing (via the wearer's sweat) through the wearing of a bracelet or anklet. Some such monitoring devices combine a number of biometric tracking and surveillance technologies. For example the Soberlink company has developed digital mobile alcohol breath-testing devices that combine alcohol monitoring with facial recognition technologies for authenticating identity. The company sends text messages to clients to remind them to test their breath and send their data to designated contacts.

Other technologies available on the market are designed to assist people in tracking their sexual and reproductive functions and activities. Many apps are available for women to monitor their ovulation and menstrual cycles and to assist with achieving (or avoiding) conception. Some of these involve the input of highly detailed bodily data. For example the Glow app provides daily predictors of chance of conception and identifies fertile times on the basis of data that users input on their menstrual cycle, indicators of ovulation, intercourse, basal body temperature, cervical mucus, body mass index, cramps, use of contraception, exercise, spotting, period flow and period symptoms. The app syncs with data entered from the physical activity tracker My Fitness Pal. Glow also provides a mirror app for a woman's partner, so that the couple can track the woman's fertility as well.

Also in the realm of sexual and reproductive health and activity self-tracking, devices with motion sensors that are inserted into the vagina are sold for the purposes of helping women track their progress in strengthening their pelvic floor muscles. Developers have created monitoring devices that fit onto penises as well and are designed to measure a man's sexual activity. There are also several smartphone apps that can be used to monitor sexual activities: these apps use the sensors in the phone to monitor sound and thrusting movements when the phone is placed on the bed during sexual encounters. Some apps even calculate the calories burnt during sex and provide league tables through which men can assess their sexual prowess against other users of the app (see my more detailed analysis of these apps in Lupton, 2015c).

Various apps and devices are available for pregnant women that direct and encourage them to observe and collect detailed data about their bodies and their unborn offspring. There are numerous apps that encourage pregnant women to track such features as their diet, vitamin intake, liquid consumption, physical activity, body weight and body temperature. Several such apps contain pregnancy countdowns, so that women can see at a glance how many weeks and days along they are in the gestation timeline. Some encourage users to record their moods, feelings, cravings, appetite level and nausea as pregnancy progresses, as well as facilitating the recording of medical and test information. There are apps on the market, such as Watch Me Change, that enable women to photograph their pregnant bellies week by week and generate a time-lapse video of changes over time as their bumps grow.

Apart from technologies focusing on bodily functions and activities, a multitude of devices and apps have been formulated that allow people to monitor and record other aspects of their lives, such as their finances, their social interactions, the use of energy in their homes, the music they listen to, the book they read, the television or films they watch and the places they visit. One of the latest self-tracking technologies is Sony's SmartBand SWR10, a digital wristband that is designed to be worn day and night. It connects wirelessly to a smartphone and also to Sony's Lifelog app, which enables the user to access other apps and platforms such as Facebook and his or her phone in order to log such aspects as places visited, music listened to, people interacted with and games played, as well as body metrics such as sleep and exercise activities.

The Reporter app can be programmed by the user to send regular questions throughout the day, in an attempt to 'illuminate aspects of your life that might otherwise be unmeasurable', such as 'Where are you?', 'Who are you with?', 'What are you doing?' and 'How do you feel?'. Users can formulate their own questions on the basis of what information they would like to collect. Apps like Swarm from Foursquare encourage people to 'check in' and update their physical location, eventually providing recommendations on places they might like to visit next. People can also use wearable or mobile devices with biosensors, in order to measure environmental conditions inside or outside such as pollution, radiation, humidity and air oxygen levels (these are often referred to as 'environmental tracking devices' or 'enviro-trackers').

Many social media sites themselves provide the quantification of users' attributes. On Twitter people's number of followers can be viewed by all users, and users themselves can check how many times their tweets are 'favourited' or retweeted by others. Facebook also displays such metrics as how many friends people have and how many comments they receive on their status updates. For some users, the 'like' button on Facebook is a powerful indicator of their popularity and social standing. Indeed some scholars have referred to the 'like economy' of Facebook (Gerlitz and Helmond, 2013). A number of apps and platforms merge social media functions with self-tracking, in an attempt to provide social support for people who are trying to achieve behaviour change or other goals. Dedicated web platforms and services for aggregating data and comparing them with others people's data are also available.

One example is the PumpUp app, which is directed at social fitness status updates. It encourages users to upload images of themselves after a workout or to demonstrate their progress towards weight loss or fitness goals, or the healthy meals they are eating – as well as enabling them to generate customised workout plans and coaching and to monitor exercise activities and progress towards their goals. The idea is both to monitor one's activities and to share them as part of encouraging positive feedback from other users, who should then act as motivating forces. Several self-help apps use the social support that may be generated by other users as part of their selling points. Apps have been developed, for example, that encourage people to construct a 'gratitude journal' in which they regularly record aspects of their lives that they appreciate (including taking photos); this journal has the function of enabling them to share the list online with others. Use of the Lift app involves creating and establishing habits and tracking progress, and it also has a social network function that allows users to provide support to others who use the app.

Gamification, or the rendering of aspects of using digital technologies and self-tracking as games, is an important dimension of new approaches to self-tracking as part of motivation strategies. Obvious examples are gaming technologies such as the Nintendo Wii Fit and the Xbox Kinect consoles (sometimes referred to as 'exergaming'). Both consoles incorporate sensors that are able to configure body metrics as part of the games they offer. Another example of gamification software is Chore Wars, which rewards users for undertaking domestic jobs by enrolling them so that they earn points. The platform gives users a fictional character and allows people in a household to track their own participation in domestic tasks and compare their data with other people sharing their house. Self-tracking apps and software adopting gamification strategies may employ such elements as built-in reward or docking systems, so that badges, points or real money can be collected or paid if various commitments – to regular exercise or weight-loss goals, for example – are either met or unmet; or they may employ websites where one's metrics can be compared competitively against those uploaded by other users. Thus, for example, the Strava running and cycling app and platform use the self-tracked data from a number of compatible GPS (global positioning system) devices. Once a run or bicycle ride has been completed, users can upload the details of their route so as to quantify and analyse their performance. An important feature of the software is the opportunity it provides for users to compare their performances with one another, in what the Strava website describes as 'social fitness – connecting and competing with each other via mobile and online apps' (Strava, 2015).

It is not only adults who use self-tracking technologies. Children are targeted for self-tracking by a plethora of software and devices in schools. Learning analytics software, for example, can supply students as well as their teachers and parents with regular reports on their learning progress. Similarly, the use of self-tracking technologies in physical education lessons may involve students accessing fitness and skill-training information that has been collected on them. Some physical education teachers require their students to wear heart-rate monitors or to use health- and fitness-related apps or coaching software that record performances for analysis. For example, the Polar GoFit app with a set of heart-rate sensors is expressly designed for physical education teachers as a monitoring tool for students' physical activities during lessons. Teachers can distribute the heart-rate sensors to students, set a target zone for heart-rate levels and then monitor these levels online while the lesson takes place – either for individuals or for the class as a group.

Platforms such as Class Dojo have also become popular in schools, particularly in the United States, where they are used by teachers as a form of behaviour monitoring and classroom control. Teachers use Class Dojo by recording aspects of their students' behaviours in class each day (how cooperative they are, how hard they work on tasks, their teamwork and so on) and send parents messages summarising these data. Students can earn points for good behaviour and lose them for non-sanctioned behaviour. They may also be encouraged to use the Class Dojo app to review their own performance. Outside the classroom there are wearable devices on the market that have been designed explicitly for children, such as the Leapfrog Leapband, which allow them to record their physical activity and earn points towards caring for a digital pet. Exergaming technologies are also promoted as ways of encouraging children to be more physically active at home and school.

The workplace has become a key site of self-tracking. Productivity-monitoring devices and software are becoming a feature of many workplaces, as employers seek to identify the habits of staff members in the interest of collecting data that will assist in maximising worker efficiency or in reducing costs. Apps designed for this purpose include RescueTime, which runs in the background of computer devices and tracks the time that users spend on applications and websites, 'giving you an accurate picture of your day' by providing detailed reports and data. Its logo is 'Measure Your Digital Life' (RescueTime, 2014). Another tool is WorkTime, a Windows app that sits in the corner of the screen and allows users to measure the time they spend on tasks. BetterWorks is one example of a social work productivity app that allows both employees and employers to track workers' progress towards achieving agreed goals and is designed to encourage employees to maintain progress, as they observe one another's information.

Many employers are also turning to the use of digital self-tracking technologies ('digital wellness tools') as part of workplace health-promotion programs or 'wellness programs'. The Virgin Pulse platform, for example, offers both productivity- and health- and fitness-tracking programs for employers (or, as the website puts it: 'Technology to replenish the modern worker'). Virgin Pulse offers a range of self-tracking services for employers to use with their workers, including wearable fitness, diet, weight, sleep and work commitment trackers. Employees receive updates on their own data and the employers view the aggregated data. Rewards and incentives for reaching goals are part of the program.

These are all designed to achieve the bottom line: 'better quality of life for your employees, and higher productivity and performance for your business' (Virgin Pulse, 2015).

There is a multitude of ways in which self-tracking technologies are used for commercial and marketing purposes. Market research companies use self-tracking apps issued to their research subjects to gauge their habits and responses, including their use of brands. The ability to send research subjects messages or prompts or to track their responses via mobile or wearable devices in real time, throughout the day, is viewed as a major development in marketing research. Mobile devices are regarded as affording the opportunity for market researchers to make 'passive data collection' – that is, data that are automatically generated by the device (such as geolocation details of users, how long they engage in activities and with whom they interact) – and 'participative data collection' – by asking users to respond to questions or prompts through their mobile devices (this is also referred to as 'push' requests). Both kinds of data can be combined; for example, the location of users can be identified, and then 'push' requests can be issued to them on the basis of where they are and what they are doing at the time (Poynter, 2014).

Emotion tracking has become an area of interest for marketing research. For example, Studio XO has developed XOX, an 'emotional technology' program that enables brands and artists to collect data on the emotional states of individuals in order to measure 'crowd excitement' and to tailor their products, experiences and services accordingly. The system involves a wristband embedded with sensors that collects 'intimate data' on 'levels of excitement' (XOX Emotional Technology Platform, 2014). This device is advertised as being a way not only for commercial entities and artists to harvest the emotional response of target audiences at an aggregated level, but also for people wearing it to be able to identify their own emotions. The concept is based on the idea that, as audiences or target groups are experiencing an event or using a brand, they will also be able to view the collective emotional responses of others in visual form, thus heightening their own experience. Artists and developers of brands will be able to measure group emotional engagement by using the same data.

Self-tracking devices are also becoming incorporated into projects that seek to enhance users' mood, happiness and social relationships. Some designers are working with experimental technologies and investigating their potential. For example, a team at Newcastle University has developed the prototype of an acoustic monitor that is worn on the arm and measures the quality and quantity of social interactions as part of determining the wearer's psychosocial wellbeing. The actual words used are not recorded. Rather the device collects such data as frequency and length of interaction and voice acoustic properties such as pitch and amplitude – indicators of emotional state according to the researchers. The device will be piloted by clinicians working with people with depression (Open Lab, 2011).

Designers who work for the nytlabs – that is, the New York Times R&D (research and development) Lab – are experimenting with prototypes of wearable devices that they dub 'social wearables/augmentation' (Feehan, 2014). One example is Blush, an object worn like a brooch. Blush listens to conversations with and around the wearer and lights up when the conversation refers to topics that the user has listed in the associated app. The researchers of Intel Labs are investigating ways of sharing with others personal data derived from self-tracking so as to contribute to social relationships and empathy. Drawing on such bodily indices as galvanic skin response (electrical changes in the skin) and heart rate in wearers of digital devices, these researchers are attempting to develop algorithms that can interpret physiological responses as moods. They are also developing technologies that allow users to transmit their experiences and physical sensations directly to others by using such indicators as the colour of their own clothing (which transmit their physiological reactions or responses), so that other people can more easily understand how these users are feeling (Intel IT Center, 2014).

While the array of wearable self-tracking devices has proliferated, many objects or environments have embedded sensors that are not inserted in, worn on or carried by the human body but only touched by it, being located in the physical surroundings in which a person moves, sits or lies: furniture, floors, cars, bicycles, toys, fridges, shopping centres, roads, airports, schools and so on. Urban environments – the so-called 'smart cities' – are becoming equipped with sensors, cameras and other digital data-gathering technologies. These generate information that is displayed with the help of real-time interactive visualisations and digital dashboards; and these in turn assist citizens, policymakers and managers to easily access and read this information. A number of these 'smart' objects (also called 'anti-wearables') provide capacities for self-monitoring. Some 'smart cars', for example, now have sensors that monitor driving habits and heart rate to identify drowsiness, alerting drivers if they are at risk of falling asleep at the wheel. Smart cars have also become incorporated into car insurance packages. Telematic devices are installed in the car engines of drivers to track the distance they drive, their destination point and their driving style (braking habits, speed, rapid acceleration, hard cornering and so on). These data are sent wirelessly to the insurance company and are used to calculate personalised premiums.

The 'smart home' has become a feature of some people's domestic lives. Mattresses can monitor sleep patterns and body temperature, chairs and floors can sense physical movements. Smart meters can be installed to measure energy use in the home. Technologies such as the Nest platform are able to monitor inhabitants' energy use and their movements in and around this space, such as when they leave and arrive at their home. The Nest Thermostat itself learns these habits and programs accordingly. Nest has now developed partnerships with self-tracking technologies such as Jawbone, so that digital data on people's sleeping habits can be incorporated into the platform's software, allowing for the thermostat operation to be automatically linked to times of going to bed and waking up. It also offers a digital live-streaming camera, DropCam, which users can install in their homes to conduct surveillance of people and pets, checking in at any time to observe proceedings through their smart device. In essence, this results in a home that is both tracking and responding to its inhabitants.

The interconnected smart home offered by Nest is an example of the developing Internet of Things. As the Internet of Things expands further and sensor-embedded objects and environments become ever more distributed, digital objects will have even greater capacity to connect to and communicate with one another independently of human intervention, constantly creating masses of digital data on a greater number of elements of human life. Indeed some commentators contend that, instead of the Internet of Things, we should be referring to the 'Internet of Life' (Elwell, 2014).

While I have dwelt on the digital technologies for self-tracking in this chapter thus far, it is important to emphasise that nondigital methods are still used by many people (and perhaps by the majority of those who self-track) for monitoring and recording aspects of their lives. As a Pew Research Center report on self-tracking for health reasons found, while 70 per cent of the Americans whom the Center surveyed in 2012 reported that they monitored health indicators for themselves or for a loved one, most did not use digital devices to do so (Fox and Duggan, 2013). Of those who engaged in self-tracking, almost half said that they simply noted details 'in their heads', relying on their memories, while a third said that they used pen and paper. Only one fifth of self-trackers said that they used digital technologies for self-tracking health indicators.

Furthermore, self-tracking is not simply about quantified (or quantifiable) information. Material objects may be used as a form of monitoring change in one's body, state of mind or social relationships. As Susannah Fox from Pew Research put it, an old pair of jeans can provide a device by which body weight or size can be monitored: too tight, and you know you have gained weight (Montini, 2013). Not only photographs but pencil marks on door jambs have traditionally measured children's growth. Similarly a collection of baby and children's clothes may signify to a parent the growth of their children, while a set of drawings, writings by one's children, and school reports collected over time demonstrate those children's cognitive development, learning and other achievements.

Many self-trackers record nonquantifiable data as part of their practice; such data include journal accounts of their daily activities, emotional states, and relationships and collections of audio data or visual images. Several apps are available that encourage people to log their moods and emotions, their dreams, and their social relationships, focusing on qualitative features. The Shadow app, for example, allows people to describe their dreams on first waking by voice or text, while the InFlow app is designed for users to log information about their emotions and energy levels by using text descriptions and pictures rather than numbers; the aim is to discover whether there are any correlations between emotions and energy levels. The Autographer, Narrative and Ethnographer devices are tiny digital cameras that can be clipped onto the user's clothing or hung around his or her neck; they take photos continually from the wearer's perspective. In using these devices, one's focus is on collecting images that are valued for what they reveal about one's daily activities and interactions, as indicated by their visual properties rather than their metrics.

Research on self-tracking practices

Few academic research studies have yet been published on how many people are engaging in self-tracking and why they are. There has been a spate of interest in studying the phenomenon of lifelogging in human–computer interaction research. These studies were mostly directed at investigating prototypes for devices or software designed to assist in lifelogging or aimed to explain how data such as images, audio or location, collected as part of lifelogging, can assist memory. Little of this research attempted to investigate how people were using lifelogging technologies 'in the wild' and what their motivations and experiences were. Building on this work, there is now a growing collection of papers that have been published by researchers in human–computer interaction studies on self-tracking. Again, these generally take a design-oriented perspective or employ cognitive or behavioural psychological models to investigate how people interact with devices.

Most of the current research on self-tracking has been conducted by market research companies and focuses almost exclusively on people who live in the United States and who self-track for health or fitness purposes. One example is a report concerning the results of an internet survey of Americans conducted by the company TechnologyResearch in September 2014 (Graham, 2014). The company found that a quarter of the respondents said that they used either a fitness-tracking device or a smartphone app to track their health, weight or exercise. Among those who did not do so, lack of interest and concern over cost were the primary reasons that were given, although almost half of non-users said that they would use a fitness-tracking device if it were recommended or prescribed by their doctor and 57 per cent said that the possibility of lower health-insurance premiums would make them more inclined to consider wearing such a device.

A report by Nielsen found that one in six of the American adults whom this company surveyed in early 2014 used wearable devices in their daily lives. Digital fitness-tracking bands were the most popular of self-tracking devices among those who owned wearable technologies: 61 per cent owned such devices, by comparison with 45 per cent who owned smart-watches and 17 per cent who owned other mobile health devices, such as pedometers (Nielsen, 2014b). Nielsen found that young adults were more likely than older adults to own wearable devices, but men and women used them in equal numbers (Nielsen, 2014b). Men and women were nearly equally likely to wear fitness bands (women slightly more likely than men), but women were more likely to use other specialised mobile health devices (Nielsen, 2014a). Owners of wearable devices were more likely to have a high household income, particularly fitness-band owners (Nielsen, 2014b).

Yet another market research survey conducted in September 2013 found that one in ten American adults owned a digital device for monitoring physical activity, such as a Fitbit or Jawbone wearable (Ledger and McCaffrey, 2014). The survey also found that younger people mainly used these devices to improve their fitness, while older people used them for the sake of improving their health and extending their lifespan. However, in what the researchers call 'the dirty secret of wearables' (Ledger and McCaffrey, 2014: 4), it is noted that many users of physical activity wearables relinquish their use quite soon. Half of the fitness-tracker owners who were surveyed had given up using them, and a third had done so within six months of acquiring their device.

American middle-class white men with high levels of digital technological know-how are perhaps the more public face of self-tracking, particularly in their participation in and membership of the Quantified Self movement. In a study in which human–computer interaction researchers analysed 52 videos of members' talks about personal experiences of self-tracking that were posted on the Quantified Self website (Choe, Lee, Lee, Pratt, and Kientz, 2014), it was found that this demographic dominated. The presenters in most such videos were American, and particularly from the San Francisco/Mountain View/Silicon Valley area, where the Quantified Self movement was established. The vast majority of speakers were men (79 per cent), and a high proportion worked in the digital technology industry. The largest group of self-trackers in this study were monitoring health-related factors such as physical activity, food consumption, weight, and mood. Another group (comprised of software engineers and students) was interested in tracking work productivity and cognitive performance. A third group was identified, comprised of people who wanted to have new life experiences through self-tracking, which they considered to be a form of experimenting. Indeed the term 'self-experimentation' was used frequently by the speakers as relating to finding meaningful knowledge about themselves, which they could use for self-optimisation.

The self-trackers who reviewed their experiences in the videos under analysis reported many benefits of self-tracking. They noted that their health had improved or that they had successfully identified what triggered their symptoms. They also often reported becoming more aware of themselves, their social relationships and the surrounding environment. However, Choe and colleagues (2014) observed that several common pitfalls were identified in the videos: trying to track too many things; not tracking the triggers of illness symptoms; and the lack of scientific rigour in tracking approaches. Tracking too many aspects either led to people becoming weary of the process or being faced with too many data to deal with. Some participants asserted that automating one's data collection resulted in less 'tracking fatigue', as the researchers put it.

Another human–computer interaction study of American self-trackers (Li et al., 2010; Li et al., 2011) found that the reasons the participants gave for engaging in these practices were: curiosity about what their data would reveal; an interest in quantitative data and numbers in general, as part of being a 'geek'; an interest in experimenting with new tools for self-tracking; acting on a suggestion from another person; and various triggering factors – such as suffering from sleep problems, wanting to lose weight or developing an illness. This study also identified some barriers to, or difficulties in, engaging in self-tracking. These included switching between tracking strategies and therefore losing data, lacking time or motivation, forgetting to collect information, having difficulties with the methods used or with interpreting the data, or finding enough interesting information to record about oneself. Participants in the study also observed that incorporating data from different sources could be difficult, and that understanding the implications of their personal information could pose challenges.

Similar findings were evident in another content analysis of posts on the Quantified Self website: a project that sought to identify which tools members used for self-tracking and how they discussed their value and ease of use (Oh and Lee, 2015). This study found that many complaints had been raised on the website about data transfer from one device to another and problems had been discussed concerning some platforms or devices becoming discontinued, which resulted in loss of people's data. Data accuracy and the design of wearables and software were also problematic for some members. The simplicity of collecting and inputting information into self-tracking tools was a further point of discussion in members' comments. The researchers noted that members' posts were positive about their authors' sharing their own self-tracked data with other people engaged in similar pursuits, particularly in the interest of finding support and improving their motivation to achieve their objectives.

While privileged white men from Silicon Valley may dominate video talks on the Quantified Self website, there is evidence to suggest that other social groups engage in self-tracking activities. The Pew Research Center survey mentioned earlier demonstrated that women and men were equally likely to engage in self-tracking and that African Americans were more likely than non-Hispanic whites or Latinos to do so (Fox and

Duggan, 2013). In another study, based in the United Kingdom, focus group interviews with university students and junior staff members found that several of the female participants used calorie-counting apps, while some of the male participants reported using fitness-tracking apps (Dennison, Morrison, Conway, and Yardley, 2013). The participants who used such apps noted that the latter were convenient tools for them to track their own progress, to work towards goals and targets that they had set themselves and to find the motivation to achieve weight loss or better physical fitness.

People may use self-monitoring technologies to track not only their own bodies, habits and activities for personal reasons, but also those of significant others. This is particularly the case of caregivers, who may have responsibility for protecting or caring for infants or children, elderly relatives, or family members with chronic medical conditions. Fox and Duggan (2013) found that 12 percent of the Americans surveyed in the Pew Center report engaged in the monitoring of health and medical-related indicators for a loved one. Of all participants, 36 percent were caregivers; and 31 percent of these caregivers said that they tracked health indicators or symptoms in those for whom they provided care. Caregivers were also more likely to track their own health: 64 percent tracked their body weight, exercise or diet, and 39 percent tracked other health indicators or symptoms.

To date there is little published research carried out by sociologists or anthropologists who have attempted to investigate self-tracking cultures and practices empirically and from a more in-depth perspective. One example is Minna Ruckenstein's (2014) interviews with Finnish people who volunteered to wear self-tracking devices continually for a one-week period, for monitoring their heart rates and their physical activity levels. Many of her study participants found the devices reassuring and regarded them as benevolent supporters of their efforts to increase their physical activity and fitness. These participants had not used an activity- or heart rate-monitoring device before; they were healthy and not dealing with chronic illness. Ruckenstein found that people who were already regular exercisers or had an interest in monitoring technologies were particularly drawn to participating in the research, as they already had a predisposition to monitoring, measuring and comparing and wanted to be challenged by their biometric data. Participants in her study were reluctant to relinquish the device when the project had come to an end. They adopted the ethos of personal responsibility for health and wellbeing and found that these devices helped them to conform to this ideal and to manage and achieve their goals: they acted as a catalyst for change. These people expected the data produced by the devices to have an effect on them, and several commented that this indeed was the effect of wearing them. Because they knew that the devices were monitoring their physical activity, they were more likely to be active. The findings also revealed that, at least in the initial stages of wearing a device, people reported feeling more aware of their bodies than usual, although some found wearing such devices annoying. Not all of the participants found the data generated from the devices useful or interesting, but some enjoyed seeing and reflecting upon their data.

Intel Research anthropologists Dawn Nafus and Jamie Sherman (2014) engaged in ethnographic fieldwork with members of the Quantified Self movement, seeking to document the beliefs and practices that underpinned this organisation. Nafus and Sherman discovered that discourses of mindfulness and awareness of one's body and one's life were dominant at the Quantified Self Global Conference they attended. Self-tracking was represented at this forum as different from other technological practices in its intense focus on the self or the body. Nafus and Sherman discovered that the self-trackers at the conference learnt to feel their bodies or gain insights into their selves through the data that they were gathering. They often challenged accepted norms and categories about health and behaviour and what is considered relevant information through their personalised and individualised data practices.

Nafus and Sherman further observed that Quantified Self movement members tend to combine technical, community, commercial and personal objectives and often have some kind of technological, academic or medical background. However, the emphasis on personal experience in one's qualification as a Quantified Self movement member means that participants in group meetings or conferences are encouraged to relate their own reflections of using self-tracking tools rather than simply pitching ideas about devices or software that they may have developed. Against arguments that people who relinquish the use of self-tracking devices or practices are disaffected with them or do not find them useful, Nafus and Sherman adduce evidence from their fieldwork and interviews that suggests that people may do so because a new pattern of behaviour has become habituated, so that self-tracking is no longer required. In other words, by using the devices, people have achieved the self-knowledge and behaviour change they sought and no longer need them (see also Lee and Kristensen, 2015). Alternatively, self-trackers might try a different way of monitoring their behaviours or bodily functions, one that should be more relevant to their purposes.

In another study, Nafus (2014) investigated how people in London (United Kingdom) and on the West Coast (United States) used a digital home energy-monitoring system. Her focus was on how the participants in her research conceptualised and interpreted the data that these systems generated. Nafus' interviews revealed the complexities involved in making sense of the kind of information that is created by sensor-based technologies. Participants in her study commented on the need to contextualise the data that their monitoring system produced and on the work that was required from them in order for inferences to be drawn from what the sensors were telling them about their home energy use. As the interviews showed, the more the people learnt about their home energy use, the more questions were raised for them about what else they should be monitoring or about how they could compare their data with other people's data in a useful manner. They were confronted with the issue of how difficult it is to adequately monitor one's home energy use efficiency – for example how many sensors might be required, how the information generated by each sensor could be interpreted, and how these sensors might be understood in relation to each other. For many participants, the data were therefore 'dead' or 'stuck', as they were not useful or enlightening for their own purposes.

While for some people using self-tracking technologies may represent taking control of one's health, wellbeing and productivity, for others it may signify weakness, ill health or lack of self-discipline. The young English users of self-tracking health and fitness apps in the research by Dennison and colleagues (2013) mentioned that they did not want other people to know about their use, because it represented them as weak or vulnerable – in need of the assistance of such apps to achieve behaviour change. They were therefore not enthusiastic about sharing their self-monitored information with friends or family members on social media sites, as using such apps was positioned as embarrassing and socially undesirable – unless contacts on such sites were working towards similar goals and thus supporting one another. Some participants also commented on the possible negative emotional effects of not making progress and having the app constantly remind the user of this (or 'telling them off'). They asserted that such apps could be helpful when a user had a preexisting motivation, but in the absence of such motivation the apps would be irritating.

I began this chapter by outlining the evolution of contemporary self-tracking practices and by providing details of the huge range of devices and technologies that are now available to engage in these practices. The research reviewed above offers several insights into what types of people engage in voluntary self-tracking and what they gain from it. Chapter 2 will introduce some compelling theoretical perspectives that can be employed to understand self-tracking practices still further and to place them within broader social, cultural and political frameworks of meaning.

2

'New Hybrid Beings'

Theoretical Perspectives

This chapter provides an overview of social, cultural and political theory that is relevant to understanding the meanings and rationales of self-tracking cultures. I begin with discussion of what sociomaterial perspectives offer. This is followed by outlining scholarship on the topics of knowing capitalism and lively data, practices of selfhood and neoliberal politics, the cultural dimensions of embodiment, datafication, and, finally, dataveillance and privacy. All these perspectives are taken up in later chapters, where they provide insights into key elements of self-tracking cultures.

Sociomaterial perspectives

An important factor in contemporary practices of selfhood and social relations is the increasing digitisation of society and social life via a diverse array of technologies, the most obvious devices being mobile phones and social media. Life is now digital (Lupton, 2015a). As Deuze (2011: 137) asserts, the spread of media, particularly digital media, into most avenues of everyday life is so extensive that we should now not talk about living '*with* media' but rather '*in* media', and we are therefore 'living a *media life*' (2011: 138). Digital devices are incorporated into our everyday routines, entangled with our sense of self, our experience of embodiment, our acquisition of knowledge and meaning making and our social relations. Whether or not we choose to take up digital technologies such as smartphones, the extent to which digital devices and sensors are embedded in public spaces and social institutions means that we cannot easily escape becoming a subject of digitisation. Public and private spaces are now reconfigured by computer code. The sheer mobility and pervasiveness of contemporary digital devices and the fact that we can connect to the internet and thus to our online social networks from almost anywhere and at any time have had a major effect on the conduct of everyday life.

To fully understand the processes by which this is happening, theorising the nature of humans' intertwinings with technologies is required. Perspectives that focus on the materialities of human action and meaning have become an important dimension of contemporary sociocultural theory. Such approaches – often referred to as 'new materialisms' or 'sociomaterialism' – go beyond the emphasis on language and discourse that was central to poststructuralism, to acknowledging the role played by material objects in social life and in concepts of selfhood and embodiment (Coole and Frost, 2010; Gillespie, Boczkowski, and Foot, 2014). Sociomaterialism has been strongly influenced by science and technology studies, and in particular by the actor–network theory approach, which focuses on the ways in which human actors interact with nonhuman actors as part of heterogeneous and dynamic social networks. Objects are considered to be agents in these networks and to have the capacity to exert influence on the other actors, including humans (Latour, 2005; Law and Hassard, 1999). Sociomaterialist scholars are therefore interested both in things and meanings and in how these relate. Objects are represented as participating in specific sets of relations, including relations with other artefacts as well as people. This approach also acknowledges the wider contexts in which object–subject relations are configured – contexts such as geographical location, age, gender, ethnicity and socioeconomic status – and the influence of these relations upon contexts.

Building on this approach, a sociomaterial position on any kind of human use of technology emphasises the multiplicity and constantly changing aspects of the subject–object relationship. Proponents of the approach address such issues as the ontological nature of the human–technology interaction (that is, how people experience technologies), the ways in which technologies are incorporated into concepts of embodiment and selfhood, how they extend or enhance these concepts, and how social relations are configured through, with and by technologies. They also emphasise that a large and complex network lies behind the technologies that people use; this network includes technology developers and makers as well as the economy and modes of sale, distribution, advertising and marketing (see, for example, Bijker, Hughes, Pinch, and Douglas, 2012).

The sociomaterial approach as it has been applied to digital technologies views the software that structures and manages the interactions and networks that take place through and with these devices as being themselves the products of social interactions – decisions made by their developers and coders. It also emphasises the materiality of digital technologies, including that of the digital data generated from the users' interactions with the technologies (Aslinger and Huntemann, 2013; Gillespie et al., 2014; Mackenzie, 2005; Manovich, 2013). The approach is relevant to understanding how things in our lives – such as digital objects – are appropriated for everyday practices, how meaning and significance are invested in objects, and what the affective dimensions of this process may be.

The concept of assemblage is often used in the sociomaterialism literature. An assemblage is configured when humans, nonhumans, practices, ideas and discourses come together in a complex system (Marcus, 2006). With digital technologies it is the case that computer software and hardware developers, manufacturers and retailers, software coders, algorithms, computer servers and archives, the computing cloud, websites, platforms and social media sites are all part of the network of actors that configure and enact a range of assemblages. Several different types of assemblage are configured via the interactions of humans and digital nonhumans. One such assemblage is the human-body–device–sensor–software–data configuration that is generated when people use a digital device to monitor and measure their physical activities. This assemblage may also incorporate other human and nonhuman actors – for example when users share their personal data with one another or attempt to synchronise the data across other devices or platforms, or when many users' data are aggregated and rendered into large data sets, which may in turn be employed for a range of purposes by other human actors.

The ways in which people incorporate objects into the routines of their everyday lives – or effectively how they become entangled in assemblages with these objects – are important elements of sociomaterial investigations. Objects are transformed through this process of incorporation, becoming endowed with a biographical meaning that is specific to the living practices and spatial contexts in which these objects are used. But it is not a one-way process – human users are also transformed by incorporation. Such processes are inevitably relational because they involve embodied interactions and affective responses (Bell, 2004; Hartmann, 2013; Lupton, 1995a, 2015a; Turkle, 2007).

Thus, for example, smartphones are not only touched by and carried on our bodies, wearables not only sit on our wrists: they are repositories of highly personal and individualised information – images, messages, appointments, details about our bodily functions, location and activities, our friends and our family members. They are, as Turkle (2007) puts it in her title, 'evocative objects' that carry and convey memories and emotions and remind us of our histories and social relationships. They bear the marks of our bodies as we touch and handle them. They are also invested with images of our bodies and of significant others (photographs and videos) that we may take or store in their memories. Devices that are endowed with self-tracking equipment also generate, process and archive highly personal information about our bodies' functions, movements and geolocation.

Kitchin and Dodge (2011) use the term 'code/space' to denote the ways in which software and devices such as mobile phones and sensors are configuring concepts of space and identity. The data that these devices and software produce structure our notions of identity and embodiment, our relationships, our choices and preferences, and even our access to services or spaces (Andrejevic, 2013; Beer, 2009; Kitchin,

2014). They are productive in that they generate new knowledges and make contributions to such endeavours as governmental management, national security and effective policing, road and air travel safety, health and fitness promotion initiatives, education and commerce. They also work to delimit and shape the capacities of individuals, and it is in this sense that they play a disciplinary and constraining role (Kitchin and Dodge, 2011).

Knowing capitalism and lively data

Theorists who have written on the emergence of the global digital data economy have pointed out that power now operates through modes of communication (Castells, 2000; Kitchin, 2014; Lash, 2007; Lyon and Bauman, 2013; Thrift, 2005). Nigel Thrift (2005) uses the phrase 'knowing capitalism' to denote this new form of global economy. Knowing capitalism depends both on technologies that generate knowledge in the form of digital data in massive quantities and on the commodification of these knowledges. It also rests on the valuing and promotion of innovation, for which new knowledges are required. Digital data have become highly valuable and commercially profitable as forms of knowledge, particularly when they are aggregated into big data sets (such a set is commonly referred to as 'big data'). Because of their volume, detail and continuous production, big data are often represented as 'disruptive' and 'revolutionary' forms of information. They have been described as offering unprecedented potential to generate insights into human behaviours, public services, healthcare and public health, security and policing, agriculture, education, workplace productivity, global development, the economy, and environmental conditions (Kitchin, 2014; Lupton, 2015a).

The actions of digital technology users and the behaviours that are tracked via their routine encounters with these technologies are integral to the digital data economy. An important element is the shift from commodifying workers' bodily labour to profiting from information collected on people's behaviours, habits and preferences. Some commentators in internet studies use the term 'prosumption', a neologism that combines the words 'production' and 'consumption' (Ritzer, 2014). This term denotes the ways in which people interacting with online technologies and other digital devices simultaneously consume and create digital content. One form of content is the routinely generated information that is created when people go online: making calls and texts on smartphones, engaging in online shopping, opting in to consumer loyalty programs that track their purchases in store, using search engines, browsing the internet, uploading apps that automatically track information on geolocation and other details of users – and so on. Another form of content is generated when users of digital technologies deliberately contribute information or comments, such as when they upload status updates, comments, audio-files or images to social media sites, click on 'like', 'favourite', 'retweet' or 'share' buttons, comment on other people's updates and posts or write blog posts.

The notion of personal data as commodities is now frequently articulated in commercial circles. As the common expression has it, the user of online technologies is 'the product'. The fine-grained details that prosumption generates about people's habits and preferences allows for targeted advertising. The value of the data that prosumption produces explains why so many services such as social media platforms and apps are offered for free. An entire industry has developed around harvesting big data and finding profitable ways of using and selling them. The 'internet empires' – the likes of Google, Apple, Facebook, Microsoft and Amazon – exert tremendous power by virtue of their ownership and control over digital data in the global information economy (Kitchin, 2014; Lash, 2007; Van Dijck, 2013). Hackers have also profited from the value of personal data, a fact that led to the incidence of many cases of illegal access to digital data sets and to the selling of these data on the black market (Ablon, Libicki, and Golay, 2015).

Central to portrayals of the digital data economy is the idea that digital data are lively, mutable and hybrid. Metaphors of liquidity are very commonly used to describe the contemporary nature of digital data: 'flows', 'streams', 'rivers', even 'floods' and 'tsunamis' are terms that recur, particularly in accounts of big data (Lupton, 2015a). In the digital data economy, flows of information are generated that are engaged in nonlinear movement. Once these flows are generated, they enter into a digitised space in which they circulate and move between different sites, being repurposed and contributing to new data assemblages (Beer, 2013; Lash, 2006; Lyon and Bauman, 2013). As Thrift (2014) contends, 'new hybrid beings' are created by the mixtures between material objects with data and bodies. Bodies and identities are fragmented into a series of discrete components, as digital data, and reassembled through this process of reconfiguration. Such digital assemblages then become targeted for various forms of intervention: personal, managerial, governmental or commercial.

As I noted in the Introduction, the notion of lively data captures these vital characteristics of digital data, as well as acknowledging that, as recordings of human activities and bodies, such data are about human life (and indeed often about nonhuman life, for example about the animals and plants that are part of agricultural industries). Furthermore, digital data and the algorithmic analytics that are used to interpret them and to make predictions and inferences about individuals and social groups are beginning to have determining effects on people's lives, influencing their life chances and opportunities. Therefore digital data both are sociomaterial artefacts generated and stored by digital technologies and have potential sociomaterial effects. Not only are these data themselves mobile, so are many of the devices that generate them: the smartphones, iPads, iPods and wearable technologies that can readily be carried around on the body from place to place and connect to the internet in almost any location. Furthermore, as people enter and exit sensor-embedded spaces, more types of digital data are generated. Thus personal data can be generated from multiple locations, as people move from space to space carrying or wearing their mobile devices.

This circulation of knowledge is also characterised by flux. Digital data do not always move freely. There are resistances and blockages (Lash, 2006). As Nafus (2014) put it in the title (see Chapter 1), data may be experienced as 'dead' or 'stuck', offering little of value in terms of insights. These blockages may include internet companies' increasing ownership of digital data archives and the inability of many of the people who generated these data to gain access to them (Andrejevic, 2014). They may also include digital users' lack of knowledge about what happens to their personal data once they have been uploaded to the computing cloud and how to interpret materialisations of their data.

Data materialisations constitute an important dimension of knowing capitalism, as they are ways of rending small pieces of information into forms that can be understood and used. If the digital data economy is conceptualised as comprised of fluidities and fluxes of data, by extending this metaphor it could be asserted that, through the process of generating data representations and visualisations, the data themselves are made 'solid', their liquidities 'frozen' at certain points. Thus, for example, the bidimensional (2D) materialisations of digital data that are generated by software – graphs, lists of numbers and other visual representations – render these data fixed at a certain point in time. Artefacts that are fabricated from digital data sets printed from 3D printers are even more literally 'solid' digital data objects, as they can be touched and held.

When 2D data visualisations are created, much emphasis is placed on their aesthetic quality, as well as on their ability to convey information in forms easy to understand. The choices that are made about which data to select and how to represent them structure the meaning of the subsequent visualisation (McCosker and Wilken, 2014). So, too, 3D materialisations of digital data represent the outcome of a series of human decision-making activities concerning the best ways to model such data, the kinds of materials that should be used and the size of the resultant object. These decisions are structured within the affordances of the software and hardware that are available for the process; and they are mediated through human expertise in handling these nonhuman elements. While the ultimate aim is to generate a useful, aesthetically pleasing and meaningful object, there are many contingencies and some messiness to confront as part of the process.

Practices of selfhood and neoliberal politics

Social theorists who have reflected on the nature of selfhood also offer much to the development of an understanding of self-tracking cultures. Three interrelated dimensions of Michel Foucault's theorising of selfhood and citizenship are relevant. The first is his writings on the practices of selfhood; the second is his concept of governmentality via biopolitics, or the ways in which citizens and societies are managed by 'soft' power that emphasises their own responsibility; and the third is his work on power and surveillance.

Foucault's writings on the discourses and practices of self-hood note that the self is fashioned through and with the articulation of power and intersections of discourses and practices (Foucault, 1986, 1988). As he was able to demon-strate in his histories of selfhood, practices of the self are culturally and historically contingent: different eras privilege different ideas and discourses about how citizens should conduct themselves. Foucault contended that it is through the practices directed at the care of the self, body and soul that people internalise ideas about appropriate conduct as members of society. In contemporary western societies, the care of the self is viewed as an ethical project, which requires a self-awareness based on critical and considered reflection and the acquisition of self-knowledge as part of achieving the ideal of the 'good citizen' – that is, a citizen who is respon-sible, capable and self-regulated in the pursuit of happiness, health, productivity and wellbeing.

Adopting another perspective on concepts of selfhood in western societies, sociologists Anthony Giddens, Ulrich Beck and Zygmunt Bauman have written, more specifically, about how individuals are dealing with the uncertainties, loss of traditional norms, and risks that are central features of life today (see, for example, Bauman, 2000; Beck, 1992, 1999; Giddens, 1991). All three sociologists make reference to the state of late modernity – that is, the contemporary era in developed societies – and to the development of reflexivity as part of the experience of people living in these societies today. Giddens, Beck and Bauman emphasise that self-reflexivity – seeking information and making choices about one's life in a context in which traditional patterns and frameworks that once structured the life course have largely dissolved – is part of contemporary practices of selfhood. Rather than conform-ing to established traditions, people must choose from an array of options when deciding how to shape their lives.

Because they must do so, their life courses have become much more open, but also much more subject to threats and uncertainties. People are compelled to make themselves central to their own lives when they take on the ethical project of selfhood. This is taking place in a political context of the developed world – that of neoliberalism – that champions self-responsibility, the market economy and competition and where the state is increasingly withdrawing from offering economic support to citizens.

These ideas converge with those expressed in Foucault's writings on the care of the self in their emphasis on the ways in which people must work to engage in self-reflection and to acquire self-knowledge, and must take responsibility for the outcomes of their lives. Beck, Giddens and Bauman, as well as other scholars who have drawn on their work, contend that we are currently in an age of reinvention of the self and the body. The concept and practices of reinvention have become central to both private lives and organisations, and it is generally accepted that such practices are important endeavours. Reinvention is about transformation for the sake of personal growth, achievement, career success, health or wellbeing. Cosmetic surgery or major weight loss are perhaps the most obvious reinvention practices, but others include seeking advice from psychologists or life success coaches, reading self-help books, retraining, changing careers or moving to new cities or countries (Beck, 1992; Beck and Beck-Gernsheim, 1995; Elliott, 2013a, 2013b). Elliott (2013a) argues that there is a deep cultural fascination with self-reinvention, as well as institutional pressures that encourage people to adopt this perspective. An expectation of instant transformation is part of the self-reinvention ideal, as is the notion that transforming the self will alleviate anxieties and fears about one's destiny.

For some commentators, the reflexive practices of selfhood can descend into vanity and narcissism. In his book *The Culture of Narcissism*, Christopher Lasch (1991 [1979]) contends that the modern era is characterised by overt and extreme forms of narcissism, in which, as part of competitive individualism, people focus on themselves to the exclusion of devoting attention to the wellbeing and welfare of others. A more recent analysis of the sociocultural dimensions of vanity in the early twenty-first century remarks on the diverse ways in which people engage in practices that are directed at enhancing their appearance, productivity or social standing – from fitness, wellbeing and anti-ageing activities to interactions on social media sites (Tanner, Maher, and Fraser, 2013). Tanner and colleagues point out that the notion of vanity has gradually changed since Lasch first wrote his book. Expectations from people that they engage in self-optimisation have led to such practices becoming more accepted instead of being viewed pejoratively, as 'vain'. Such practices of selfhood are now frequently represented as expected from people and as part of their achieving their 'best selves' and behaving as responsible citizens, engaged in self-care. In some contexts, engaging in self-optimisation or enhancement is even demanded of people (for example, public health campaigns exhort people to give up smoking or lose weight). In some ways, therefore, contemporary concepts of selfhood require a degree of self-preoccupation. The boundaries between self-reflexivity, vanity and narcissism are not always easily defined. It is still deemed important, however, to strike an appropriate balance between working to optimise the self and not appearing to others overly self-absorbed.

The development of certain forms of expert-knowledge systems has been vital in configuring dominant ideas about how practices of selfhood should be conducted. Foucault (1988) identifies four types of technologies that produce knowledge about human life: (1) technologies of production, which allow people to produce, transform or manipulate material objects; (2) technologies of sign systems, which involve the production and manipulation of symbols, images, ideas and discourses; (3) technologies of power, which determine people's conduct and submit them to certain ends; and (4) technologies of the self, which permit people to engage in their own practices of selfhood, in pursuit of their own interests. Foucault notes that these technologies tend to work together to produce forms of knowledge about humans, but each relies upon certain modes of training and modification of people, including the inculcation of practices and ways of thought. His objective was not to accept these knowledges at face value but to investigate the rationalities and what

Foucault calls the 'truth games' that underpin the techniques that people use in understanding themselves.

Over the past century, the psy disciplines (psychology, psychiatry, psychotherapy, psychoanalysis) have come to play a dominant role in understandings of selfhood. Theories and models of human behaviour and identity, as they are articulated in psychology and psychiatry, structure and discipline norms and make prescriptions for how people should act to improve their mental health, overall wellbeing and general success in life (Rose, 1996). Many of these ideas have disseminated into mass culture in the form of self-help and popular psychology books (and now websites and apps). The self-help industry is overtly directed at using psychological models of human behaviour to assist people in maximising their opportunities. The materials that contribute to the self-help literature reproduce the notion of individuals as atomised actors who are expected and encouraged to work upon themselves in the quest to achieve health, productivity and happiness. The authentic or true self is represented as ontologically separate from the inauthentic self and as an entity that can be worked on by the self for the self through practices such as introspection and self-reflection. In this literature it is typically contended that one should have a relationship with one's self that involves an ethical responsibility to achieve this authentic self. Such a relationship involves delving beneath the surface in order to uncover the hidden desires, drives and motivations that the psyche harbours (Elliott, 2013a; Hazleden, 2003; Keane, 2000). Part of this practice requires self-monitoring – noticing aspects of one's thoughts, feelings and relationships and taking steps to intervene if negative thoughts or experiences are identified. This process of self-monitoring may involve answering a questionnaire or writing down thoughts and feelings regularly for perusal and reflection (Hazleden, 2003).

While these practices of selfhood may appear to be highly individualistic, broader issues of power and the government of citizens underpin their rationales. As scholars drawing upon Foucault's (1991) work on governmentality have contended, this political approach promotes the concept of the citizen who needs no coercion to behave productively and in the interests of the state. Neoliberal political rationalities generally rely on apparatuses of 'soft' rather than 'hard' power. Instead of relying on coercive measures that appear to be imposed from above, in managing and regulating their citizens neoliberal political systems invest faith in the voluntary take-up of imperatives by the citizens themselves. Citizens believe that certain acts are in their own best interest or are integral to ideal selfhood; thus they engage willingly in these acts (Burchell, Gordon, and Miller, 1991; Rose, 1990). For example, people attempt to become productive workers or to engage in health-promoting behaviours because they see it as a way towards achieving their optimal selves (Kelly, 2013; Lupton, 1995b).

Such an approach combines the ethos of the care of the self (or of governing the self) with that of the ideal citizen (governing over populations). Individuals can be regarded as fulfilling their obligations as citizens if they devote attention to optimising their own lives. Simultaneously they are engaging in practices of freedom, since they are oriented towards achieving personal goals. Such practices appear to be emerging from personal desires and voluntary objectives related to the achievement of health, happiness and success rather than from imperatives issued by the state or other sources of authority. In the discourses that champion the ideal of the rational neoliberal citizen, social structural factors that influence people's living conditions and life chances – such as social class, gender, geographical location, race and ethnicity – are discounted in favour of the notion that people are self-made.

In self-help discourses it is assumed that such goals do not come naturally but must be worked towards, with the assistance of an expert who gives advice and through endeavours on the part of the individual concerned. Such discourses appeal to the notion that people are rational beings who would naturally want to achieve these goals and to make the corresponding effort. Optimising the self and one's life trajectory is simply a matter of applying knowledge effectively. This logic assumes that, once the appropriate knowledge is gained and applied, most problems and difficulties can be resolved. Any suggestion that a person's difficulties may be caused by intractable biological problems (a genetic predisposition towards illness, for example) or by their position as members of socially or economically disadvantaged groups tends to be discounted for the sake of this focus on personal management and responsibility. Not overcoming difficulties becomes firmly positioned as the fault of the private individual rather than of their relative social and economic advantage.

Cultures of embodiment

The nexus of human bodies, digital devices, sensor-embedded spaces and data offers some intriguing possibilities for thinking through the contemporary experience of the digitised human. Bodies are now increasingly digitised in a multitude of ways – from the digital scanning technologies that the medical clinic uses in order to observe, monitor, diagnose and treat diseases to the selfies that are posted to Facebook, the videos that are uploaded to YouTube and the types of digital self-tracking apps and devices that were described in Chapter 1.

Self-tracking beliefs and practices may be viewed as simply one approach among the many that have been used across the millennia to control, manage, regulate, perform and express embodiment. For social theorists who have written about the body, the ways of thinking about the body and of living in it and acting on it are all culturally, socially and historically contingent. One important element of self-tracking practices in relation to embodiment is how we control and manage our bodies. In contemporary western societies, mind and body tend to be regarded as separate entities. Ideally, in the pursuit of self-knowledge and self-improvement, the mind is able to exert control over the body. In this understanding of the body, it is viewed as a possession of the self, needful of careful training and discipline. The body, therefore, is regarded as also reflecting the capacity for self-discipline of and knowledge of the self that inhabits the body (Leder, 1990; Longhurst, 2000; Lupton, 1995b, 2012, 2013a; Shilling, 1993).

Foucault emphasised the importance of the human body as a site of power enactments and struggles, and this is central to his concept of biopower. Biopower involves both a focus on the bodies of individuals and how they manage and regulate their bodies as part of their everyday lives, and on the monitoring, management and promotion of the welfare of populations (or the body politic). Rather than disciplinary power being exerted on individuals or populations, biopower is far more subtle, focused on the promotion of self-regulation and self-management (Foucault, 1979; 1984). The related term biopolitics refers to the diverse ways in which biopower is exerted, not only by government authorities but by the range of other agencies that focus on humans' bodies and behaviours, such as commercial and research enterprises.

Symbolic ideas about the control of the body politic are intertwined with those that structure the way people think about human bodies. Related to these understandings of the appropriate deportment of the body are ideas about bodily containment and management that in western societies have traditionally privileged rigid control of the body, its size and shape, its activities and functions. Bodily containment is linked to moral meanings associated with binary oppositions such as thin/fat, healthy/ill and normal/pathological. The body that is unable to be contained, over which its owner seems to have little control, is an object of pity, ridicule and disgust. In contrast the tightly contained body, associated with a lean and fit body shape, good health and vigour, is portrayed and regarded as ideal and morally just. Fat, diseased or physically unfit bodies, for example, are viewed as fleshly evidence of people's inability to exert control over their bodily urges and desires or their ignorance about how they are damaging their bodies (Longhurst, 2000; Lupton, 1995b, 2012, 2013b).

As part of seeking to achieve the ideal of the tightly contained body, the body's boundaries and its leaks and flows must be monitored. Cultural theorists such as the anthropologist Mary Douglas (1966) have argued that the regulation of the flow of phenomena inside and outside the body and the establishment and maintenance of boundaries between the inside and the outside are vital conceptual practices across human societies. Symbolic and social practices and concepts work to operate and police the boundaries of the body politic and to deal with threats that are viewed as challenging the stability and order of this body.

The metaphors that underpin understandings and practices of embodiment reveal the preoccupations of the era in which people live. The metaphor of the body as machine has a long history in western culture (Lupton, 2012). This metaphor changes as the technologies that dominate in historical eras change. At the time of the Industrial Revolution, for example, the human body was frequently portrayed as an engine, with pistons and pumps. With the advent of computer technologies, the body has often been represented as part of a digital information system, subject to communication errors causing illness and disease (Haraway, 1991; Hayles, 2008; Lupton, 1995a, 2012). There has also been a move from haptic ways of knowing the body (that is, ways that rely on the sense of touch) to visual knowledges. Technologies for screening and diagnostic purposes such as x-rays, computer tomography, ultrasound and magnetic resonance imaging have been used for some decades to monitor, record and interpret the body, to gaze into and produce images of its interior. In recent times digital technologies have become increasingly important to the visualisation and display of the human body in medicine (Cartwright, 1995; Duden, 1993; Waldby, 1997).

Part of this increasing use of visualising technologies is a significant shift in how the body and health states are conceptualised, articulated and portrayed. Where once people relied upon the sensations they felt in their bodies and reported to their physicians, medical technologies devoted to producing images of the body have altered the experience and treatment of bodies. The optic has come to take precedence over the haptic in revealing the 'truth' of the body (Duden, 1993). Such technologies produce a virtual patient, a 'screen body'. The visual image or the data they generate are often privileged as more 'objective' than the signs offered by the 'real', fleshly body and the patients' own accounts of their bodies (Chrysanthou, 2002; Rich and Miah, 2009; Waldby, 1997).

Digital devices are able to extend the capacities of the body by supplying data that can then be used to display the body's limits and capabilities and allow users to employ these data to work upon themselves and present themselves in certain ways. Writing before the advent of these devices, Chrysanthou (2002) noted the move towards individuals using information and computer technologies such as online health assessments, over-the-counter diagnostic tests and self-administered genetic tests, as part of what he describes as a

utopian vision of the perfect, imperishable body. These technologies participate in a kind of 'techno-utopia', in which
technologies are positioned as harbingers of progress, keys to
the promotion of human happiness, wellbeing and health
(Davis, 2012). Like medical imaging technologies, mobile
digital technologies that measure bodily movement and body
functioning and report these data to the device user and to
those with whom the user chooses to share them produce a
spectacular body, one in which the internal workings are
similarly displayed and made visible. As part of the project
of seeking security and stability, such technologies attempt to
penetrate the dark interior of the body and to render it visible,
knowable and thereby (it is assumed) manageable.

Self-tracking could be described as a biometric practice
when it is devoted to the measuring and monitoring of unique
features of human bodies. The term 'biometric' refers to the
quantification of various features of the human body. Biometric data have becoming increasingly used in forms of inclu-
sion and exclusion and in the maintenance of borders and
other boundaries. In the discourse of biometric surveillance
technologies, the body becomes represented as a site of information, made up of data flows and circulations. Indeed the
body and the data it represents become central to concepts
of identity. Here the distinction between the body as 'thing'
and the digital representation of that 'thing' is levelled out
(Ajana, 2013). The body is viewed as a repository of identifiable, storable and processable data via such techniques as
genetic screening, fingerprinting, retina and facial imaging,
and so on (Ajana, 2013; van der Ploeg, 2003). Biometric
practices translate bodies into readable texts and valorise the
digitisation of bodies (van der Ploeg, 1999). They digitally
mediate between the body and identity and between technology and identity (Ajana, 2013). Turning fleshly sensation,
behaviour and perception into digitally produced numbers
becomes a way of mastering the uncertainties, inaccuracies
and vagaries of human embodiment.

Datafication

Now that bodies and selves, social life, social institutions and
spaces are increasingly monitored digitally and configured by

digital technologies that document and record data, the meanings and uses of these data have become important topics of enquiry. A body of literature that may be loosely described as critical data studies (Kitchin and Lauriault, 2014) has begun to develop in response to recent popular representations of digital data, both 'small' and 'big'. In countering mainstream portrayals of big data, critical data scholars have drawn attention to the ways in which data are social and cultural artefacts, configured via human decision-making and underpinned by tacit assumptions. The view that 'data are never raw' – that is, they are always 'cooked' via social, cultural and political frames and practices (Gitelman and Jackson, 2013) – is relevant to any form of data. Critical data studies scholars emphasise the role played by the internet corporations and other digital developers in shaping how data are gathered, analysed and employed and the power relations that are inherent in these processes. They also explore the nature of the social relations that are configured by and enacted with digital data (Andrejevic, 2013, 2014; Beer and Burrows, 2013; boyd and Crawford, 2012; Kitchin, 2014).

The process of 'datafication' – that is, of rendering complex human behaviours, feelings, relationships and motivations into forms of digital data (van Dijck, 2014) – often involves metricisation, which means converting these aspects of life into numbers. This valorisation of quantified data may be viewed as yet another dimension of the importance of quantification and metrics in underpinning technologies of biopower. Expert knowledges on human life are essential to biopolitics, as they provide the truth claims by which people are invited or expected to take up certain body-related practices and interventions (Lupton, 1995b; Rose, 2007, 2008). Statistical data were important to the strategies of normalisation as they emerged in the nineteenth century, because they rendered bodies more visible and manageable and constructed norms by which individuals could be compared (Hacking, 1990). Statistics and other forms of metricisation of humans' habits, thoughts and functions are even more important to contemporary strategies and apparatuses of biopower and biopolitics.

Sociologists have begun to direct attention at the ways in which questions of measure and value permeate now many aspects of social life (Adkins and Lury, 2011; Burrows, 2012; Day, Lury, and Wakeford, 2014; Ruppert, 2011). They argue that numerical data collected on populations, in particular, are a specific means of constructing certain metric assemblages of individuals or populations from a variety of sources. The metrics derived from digital databases lend visibility to aspects of individuals and groups that are not otherwise perceptible, because such metrics are able to 'join up' a vast range of details derived from diverse sources. Individuals and social groups or populations are thereby rendered into multiple aggregations that can be manipulated and changed in various ways, depending on the aspects focused upon or searched for. Behaviours and dispositions are interpreted and evaluated with the help of the measuring devices, complex algorithms and opportunities for display afforded by these technologies, all of which allow for finer detail to be produced about individuals and populations. These metrics may be used to make assessments about the performance of people, groups and things like government agencies or schools – or, in the case of medicine, healthcare services or therapies.

We are entering an era in which biopolitics and the expert knowledges that underpin biopower have become increasingly digitised. In a world in which regimes of truth are frequently configured through the algorithmic processing of digital data (Harsin, 2015; Lash, 2007; Thrift, 2005), such data are frequently represented as neutral and highly accurate forms of information that promise to offer insights into social, economic and environmental phenomena. Digitised data exert a particular authority over other sources of information about oneself or others because they are viewed as more objective, detailed, 'in the moment' and readily able to integrate information from many different sources. Unlike the allegedly subjective information that people receive from their senses and through observations, digital data carry with them an aura of scientific authority. Computer codes, software and the data that they generate offer a late modernist promise of exerting control over messy, undisciplined scenarios. They offer the (illusory) power of automatically enforcing what they prescribe, doing away with human subjectivity and its resultant inaccuracy and bias (Hui Kyong Chun, 2011). These representations of data view them as objects that preexist discovery, waiting to be identified, collected and used for a specific purpose, generated by machines rather than people. Harsin (2015: 4) refers to the 'truth markets' that are generated and supported by digital data. These markets are fragmented and dispersed among a wide variety of organisations that stretch far beyond state-governed apparatuses. They are all underpinned by big data analytics.

When discussing the contributions of digital technologies to neoliberal political rationalities and practices, some scholars have focused more specifically on algorithms and on the ways in which these elements of software act to make social distinctions and judgements, exerting 'algorithmic authority' (Rogers, 2013) in an increasingly wider sphere of influence. In structuring computer decision-making, algorithms serve to shape beliefs about what type of data are important and relevant and how they should be combined to produce knowledges. The algorithms constructed by software coders bring digital data together in certain ways, which result in algorithmic identities that are configured on behalf of users (Cheney-Lippold, 2011).

These algorithmic identities can have material effects. Increasingly algorithms play an integral role in defining access to information and in generating predictions about how people will behave, and this fact has accompanying implications for the opportunities or constraints with which people may be presented. It has therefore been contended that algorithms, through their power to intervene in decision-making about the life chances of individuals, have contributed to the soft power of contemporary neoliberal governance. In the face of the rapidly growing influence of this algorithmic authority, it is difficult to challenge it, given that the coding that structures algorithms is generally 'black-boxed' and unavailable for direct interrogation (Cheney-Lippold, 2011; Gillespie, 2014; Neyland, 2015; Totaro and Ninno, 2014).

Dataveillance and privacy

The continual generation of digital data about individuals who use online technologies provides the opportunity for this information to be used to monitor people; this can be done either by the people themselves, at their own will and on their own behalf, or by other actors and agencies. The term 'surveillance' is often employed in relation to the ways in which digital technologies operate. This word tends to suggest an authoritative form of monitoring, which is exerted from above on disempowered or unknowing subjects. Yet there are many versions of surveillance – or, as some theorists would prefer, 'veillance' (which simply refers to 'watching' by its French name: *veiller*) (Lupton, 2015a). Writers in the field of surveillance studies have provided many insights into how watching operates in contemporary western societies, including through the use of digital technologies (Lyon, 2007; Lyon and Bauman, 2013). Various kinds of social relations and interactions, including power relations, are created in and through watching technologies. These technologies may be considered part of the production and governing of the citizen in neoliberal societies.

Digital technologies are often employed to facilitate a kind of surveillance that is undertaken, often by those in positions of greater authority, in order to regulate, manage and discipline people. The use of closed-circuit television (CCTV) cameras in public places, radio-frequency identification (RFID) chips in passports and identity cards and in workers' or school children's clothing and biometric screening at international borders are clear examples of such a mode of surveillance. The commercial gathering of data on internet users' routine transactions, from searching and browsing to online shopping, is also a form of standard surveillance. So too, national security agencies' watching of their citizens' online and mobile phone interactions, as revealed by the documents released by whistle-blower Edward Snowden from mid-2013, represents a type of surveillance whereby those in authority monitor the activities of others – in this case, without the latter's knowledge or consent. Digitised surveillance thus involves not only traditional forms of observing behaviours (as in the use of CCTV cameras to visually inspect people's movements), but accessing digital data and using algorithms to construct profiles on individuals in both covert and overt ways.

Panoptic surveillance is a more complex mode of watching. The Foucauldian concept of the panopticon is often employed in work on digital forms of surveillance. The panopticon is literally an architectural structure: a prison first proposed by eighteenth-century reformer Jeremy Bentham. The concept of the panopticon is used metaphorically by Foucault in his well-known work *Discipline and punish: The birth of the prison* (1977) to suggest the operations of power in contemporary societies. The panopticon metaphor emphasises the role played by the gaze, by surveillance and visibility in the new forms of power relations that emerged in the eighteenth and nineteenth centuries. The panopticon prison was a structure designed so that the monitoring gaze of those in power could operate centrally to observe inmates in their separate cells, who were unaware of when exactly they were being watched. This design allowed a small number of those in authority to watch a large number of individuals. The concept involved the idea that prisoners should not only be observed by those in authority, but also, ideally, develop self-surveillance and disciplining strategies, in an effort to improve themselves. This approach to the management of problematic populations was also taken up in relation to other institutions, such as the hospital and the school.

For Foucault, the panopticon was representative of a new form of power, one in which central surveillance and the monitoring of individuals were combined with those individuals' developing self-management techniques of their own free will. The panopticon metaphor emphasises how external rationales of surveillance may be internalised, so that people engage in self-monitoring not only because they can never be sure whether hidden others are watching them, but also because they have accepted these rationales as part of practices of the self. Thus, for example, patients who engage in self-care practices through digital monitoring systems (as part of telemedicine) are aware that their doctors and other caregivers may choose to check whether they have engaged in these routines and that their data may be sent to these people for the purposes of such surveillance. However, they may also voluntarily continue to participate in these regimens because they have accepted the importance of self-care to their practice of ideal patienthood. The power relations incipient in panoptic surveillance are therefore not merely or simply repressive. They are also productive of certain modes and practices of selfhood and embodiment.

Dataveillance is a specific type of veillance that uses digital data (Esposti, 2014; van Dijck, 2014). Dataveillance need not involve digital technologies, but one form of it occurs when digital data are collected on any interaction that people may have with internet-connected activities that generate information – either automatically, for instance when people use search engines, or intentionally, when they upload images or texts to internet sites such as social media platforms. Digital surveillance technologies differ from previous forms of watching in their pervasiveness, in the scope of the data they are able to collect and store, in their potential longevity and in the implications they have for privacy. Digitised dataveillance is a participant in the vitality of digital data and in the dispersal of digital technologies of watching, from sensor-embedded environments to sensor-embedded wearable technologies. It therefore differs from earlier modes of panoptic surveillance in that there is no centralised location from which people are watched. The distributed feature of dataveillance is emphasised in the joint work of sociologist Zygmunt Bauman with surveillance studies scholar David Lyon (Lyon and Bauman, 2013). The two use the phrase 'liquid surveillance' to describe the ceaseless monitoring of citizens with the help of digital technologies across a range of sites and for a variety of purposes.

Not only is personal information gathered via the use of digital surveillance technologies, but individuals can easily be grouped or sorted into discrete categories and classes on the basis of this information and then subjected to assessments on the basis of prior assumptions or inferences (Lyon, 2002; Lyon and Bauman, 2013). Groups that once were not subject to routine surveillance are now targeted by the dispersed liquid technologies of digital dataveillance (Haggerty and Ericson, 2000; Lyon and Bauman, 2013). Lyon (2002) employs the concept of 'surveillance as social sorting' to contend that digital surveillance operates to inform and facilitate judgements about risky individuals by constructing risk profiles and by selecting them as belonging to members of groups that impose threats to others.

Dataveillance can therefore operate so as to exclude individuals from public spaces, travel and other rights and privileges if such individuals are deemed to be posing a threat in some way. This type of social sorting is frequently discriminatory. People from specific social groups, which are categorised as undesirable by virtue of race, ethnicity or nationality, age or social class, are subjected to far more intensive monitoring, identification as 'dangerous' or 'risky', and exclusion on the basis of these factors than are those from privileged social groups (Amoore, 2011; Werbin, 2011). It has also been pointed out by critics that digital data have a much longer life and capacity to be disseminated across time and space than previous forms of surveillance. These critics have contended that the right to be forgotten is contravened by the archiving of digital data. Crimes, misdeeds and embarrassments are now perpetually available for other people to find on digital archives and databases (Bossewitch and Sinnreich, 2013; Rosen, 2012).

Several researchers have argued that the use of digital technologies may involve yet another specific type of watching: that of 'sousveillance' (Dodge and Kitchin, 2007; Kitchin, 2014; Mann and Ferenbok, 2013), which literally means 'watching from below'. In general terms, sousveillance may refer to people watching each other, as frequently occurs on social media platforms such as Facebook, Twitter, YouTube and Instagram. Indeed the very rationale of such platforms is the increased levels of visibility and watching of each other that they promote. To comment on, or even simply to look at others' content is to participate in the surveillance of others – noting what they are doing, making judgements on it and assessing its worth or interest. Indeed to be 'invisible' on social media – to post content without others noting it in some way – is undesirable. Attracting followers and comments, 'likes', 'favourites' and 'retweets' demonstrates that the content a user generates on these platforms is interesting or attractive to others (Bucher, 2012; Grosser, 2014; Helmond, 2013). Practices that were once considered coercive and imposed forms of state surveillance, such as biometric facial recognition for security purposes, are now routinely used in social media sites such as Facebook for the purposes of tagging others in images (Ellerbrok, 2011).

There are close intersections between concepts of digital surveillance and changing notions of privacy in contemporary digital society. Privacy issues have often been raised in discussions about new digital media, including social media platforms and mobile devices. Internet and legal scholars have argued that Web 2.0 technologies have had a profound effect on concepts and practices of privacy that remain in flux, as changes occur in the ways in which personal information is collected, stored and used online. Notions of privacy have been rendered complex by the social relations that are enacted on online sites and by the continuous production of digital data. Many users of social networking platforms are grappling with coming to terms with new ways of defining privacy in a context in which concepts of 'the public' and 'the private' are no longer confined to a spatial dimension. Notions of intimacy, solitude, the personal, the secret and the hidden are challenged by the confessional of social media sites such as Facebook and Twitter, in which participants' inner thoughts and private behaviours are often revealed to a large number of friends or followers, and frequently several times throughout the day. This phenomenon has been described by van Mamen (2010: 126) as 'the privatization of the public and publicization of the private'. boyd (2012) refers to the concept of 'networked privacy', which acknowledges the distributed nature of personal information and images in social media use.

It has been argued by many commentators that internet users do not expect the same kind of privacy protection that once was demanded of private communications. Some scholars have questioned whether the current era of personalised computerised technology use, social media and widespread surveillance has meant 'the end of privacy'. Have concepts of privacy narrowed down to liberal assumptions about subjectivity, are they too culturally relative or overly reliant on rights-based discourses, neglectful of new ways of living and being? Can the spatial meanings of privacy, which represent privacy as a kind of personal zone from which others are excluded unless given permission to enter, remain meaningful in a context in which digital users are available for surveillance and data gathering for much of their waking day

(Bennett, 2011; Lyon, 2010; Snow, Buys, Roe, and Brereton, 2013; Tene and Polonetsky, 2013)?

These are compelling questions that have direct relevance for self-tracking cultures and practices, particularly given the very personal and often intimate nature of the information that people collect on themselves and the growing number of domains in which this information is used by others. As I will contend in later chapters, concepts of privacy are changing again as people become more aware of the ways in which their personal digitised details are collected and used by second and third parties and of how these details may be accessed without their consent or knowledge.

One of the key arguments I make in this book is that self-tracking cultures are complex and multifaceted, and therefore require several different perspectives if we are to fully develop an understanding of their meaning and relationships to other dimensions of identity and social life. In this chapter I have offered some theoretical perspectives that provide ways of thinking about the social and cultural backgrounds and resonances of self-tracking discourses and practices. Each perspective allows scholars to explore different angles on the context of self-tracking, and what approach is found most insightful will depend on the particular aspect of self-tracking they are analysing. These perspectives will be employed at various points in the remainder of this book, as I move on to examining specific aspects of self-tracking cultures, beginning in the next chapter with how the body and the self are conceptualised and worked upon as part of self-tracking endeavours.

3

'An Optimal Human Being'

The Body and the Self in Self-Tracking Cultures

In the previous chapter some theoretical perspectives that have addressed concepts of selfhood and embodiment in contemporary western cultures were introduced. The present chapter draws on this previous discussion by examining more specifically the ways in which self-tracking cultures portray the self and the body – key foci of self-tracking endeavours. I discuss the reflexive monitoring self, representations of embodiment, the affective dimensions of self-tracking, taking and losing control, and finally selfhood and surveillance.

The reflexive monitoring self

The American television program *PBS Newshour* aired a news story on self-tracking on 28 September 2013 (the program and a full transcript are available at The quantified self: Data gone wild? 2013). The reporter began with an interview with Bob Troia, an enthusiastic self-tracker who measures his sleep patterns, pulse, blood pressure, blood glucose, cognitive performance, heart rate, sweat levels, skin temperature and stress levels using a range of devices such as his iPhone and wearable computing devices. He says that he does all this as part of attempting a healthy, enjoyable and productive life: 'Personally, like, my goal is to basically be

– an optimal human being in every aspect of my life.' The program also featured another adherent of the quantified-self approach and technology: David Pogue, columnist for *The New York Times*, who said that he engaged in self-tracking because he believed that '[y]ou want to be your best self. You want to put your best foot forward.' Pogue claimed about the quantified self: 'It's absolutely narcissism. Or more health-fully, ego. It's studying yourself as an interesting topic in ways that you couldn't study yourself before, I mean this is just giving you self-awareness into previously invisible aspects of your life.'

An article in a Finnish newspaper reported the self-tracking activities of Pekko Vehvilainen. He uses 11 different apps to record such features as his sleep patterns, body weight, body fat, heart rate and physical activity. When discussing why he engages in self-tracking, the newspaper reports Vehvilainen as commenting:

'I want to improve myself. I want to know where I am and where I'm going' ... He rolls up the sleeve of his t-shirt and points at the body analyser strapped around his arm. 'This device has taught me how to exercise and eat right,' he says ... 'Without the equipment and measurements I couldn't have reached my goals as easily.' (Heikkinen and Teivainen, 2014)

From these two news accounts, therefore, a number of discourses that give meaning to self-tracking cultures are apparent. Discourses about selfhood appear here: about the importance of self-awareness and self-improvement (the attempt to 'improve myself', be 'an optimal human being' and 'your best self') and also about the role played by self-knowledge ('studying yourself as an interesting topic', 'I want to know where I am and where I'm going'). This focus on the self and on the voluntary nature of self-tracking is also often articulated in accounts that seek to define the quantified self or the self-tracking phenomenon. As I pointed out in Chapter 1, portrayals of self-tracking in the popular media have often focused on its individualistic and apparently self-obsessed nature. Indeed some critics, such as Evgeny Morozov, have viewed digital self-tracking with a jaundiced eye. According to Morozov (2013: 223), '[t]he recent appeal of self-tracking can only be understood when viewed against the modern narcissistic quest for uniqueness and exceptionalism'.

Given that, as the terms suggest, the focus of 'self-tracking' or of the 'quantified self' is, indeed, the *self*, it cannot be denied that there is a strong emphasis on personal experience in the Quantified Self movement community. People who discuss their self-tracking practices in quantified-self forums are encouraged to talk about 'What I did, how I did it and what I learned'. In this and other self-tracking circles the concept of 'n = 1' is frequently articulated and conveys the idea that collecting data is an enterprise limited to the individual. According to the Quantified Self Institute, self-tracking 'is a functionally "selfish" activity, which is a result of a personal motivation. "Me and my data", that is the point of the Quantified Self' (de Groot, 2014). Similarly the online version of the *Oxford English Dictionary* defines self-tracking as highly personal and individualised: 'the practice of systematically recording information about one's diet, health, or activities, typically by means of a smartphone, so as to discover behavioural patterns that may be adjusted to help improve one's physical or mental well-being' (Oxford Dictionaries, 2015).

Achieving self-knowledge is an important dimension of responsible self-management. Given the affordances of new digital technologies that are positioned as able to produce ever more detailed knowledge about the self, such technologies are participants in the production of expert knowledge. People who use these technologies can generate their own expert knowledge about themselves (in the form of digital data) as well as draw on the advice offered by such digitised forms of expertise as apps and online coaches. The data collected as part of self-tracking and the patterns and associations that can be identified in and between these data are vital to this project. Understanding patterns in one's life is the starting point for making changes on the basis of these observations, and new digital technologies support this endeavour. This perspective is evident in many portrayals of the quantified self and other forms of self-tracking. In one of the earliest posts on the Quantified Self website, entitled 'What is the quantified self?', Kevin Kelly (2007) outlines his vision of the benefits of self-knowledge:

> Real change will happen in individuals as they work through self-knowledge. Self-knowledge of one's body, mind and spirit. Many seek this self-knowledge and we embrace all paths to it. However the particular untrodden path we have chosen to explore here is a rational one: Unless something can be measured, it cannot be improved. So we are on a quest to collect as many personal tools that will assist us in quantifiable measurement of ourselves. We welcome tools that help us see and understand bodies and minds so that we can figure out what humans are here for.

As Kelly's words suggest, the tools that are available for self-tracking are a central feature of practices of reflexive self-monitoring. The ethos of self-tracking dovetails neatly with that of digital entrepreneurialism, with its constant emphasis on developing or experimenting with novel technologies. The enthusiasm for consumption is evident in the Quantified Self website and other sites on self-tracking or lifelogging, where lists of devices, gadgets, software, apps and platforms that can be used for self-tracking are provided and assessments are made as to their value for self-tracking. Digital technologies afford the expansion of networks and spaces in which self-monitoring and self-management can be exercised, as well as offering new ways of gathering detailed data about individuals – data they can then use to manage and improve themselves. The devices themselves are frequently represented in self-tracking cultures as enabling technologies that not only serve to provide detailed information on the body and the self, but also act as pedagogical and motivating agents. As Pekko Vehvilainen comments: 'This device has taught me how to exercise and eat right.'

In Chapter 2 I made a reference to the importance of the psy disciplines and of the self-help ethos in contemporary understandings of selfhood. This self-help ethos is strongly evident in the self-tracking literature. Medical technologies have been presented for some time as contributing to the optimisation of the body/self for some time by controlling and improving the vital processes of embodiment and cognition (Rose, 2007). The realm of technologies of optimisation has now expanded well beyond the clinic. The contemporary 'technologies of life' that 'seek to reshape the vital future by action in the vital present' (Rose, 2007: 18) include self-tracking devices that are oriented towards recording and monitoring elements of vitality with the objective of improvement and enhancement, whether it is physical fitness or health, leisure activities, social relationships, sexual pleasure and performance, mood and mental wellbeing or work productivity.

Self-tracking may be theorised as a practice of selfhood that conforms to cultural expectations concerning self-awareness, reflection and taking responsibility for managing, governing oneself and improving one's life chances. Self-tracking therefore represents the apotheosis of the neoliberal entrepreneurial citizen ideal. Such a figure actively engages in self-improvement strategies, often involving consumption – of knowledge, objects, technologies and experiences – strategies that are viewed as enhancing self-improvement attempts. What might be described as 'the reflexive monitoring self' in the context of digitised tracking technologies is an assemblage of practices that combine regular and systemised information collection, interpretation and reflection as part of working towards the goal of becoming. Underpinning these efforts are the notion of an ethical incompleteness and a set of moral obligations concerning working on the self that are central to contemporary ideas about selfhood and citizenship.

Productivity software and apps contribute to self-tracking efforts for some people. These digitised tools enhance the notion that the ideal self is productive and efficient and makes use of time wisely and well. They convey the idea that, in a world in which people feel increasingly pressed for time, overworked and faced with many complex tasks and competing interests, digitised tools offer a solution. As the author of an online article outlining various types of apps for productivity put it: 'Who isn't looking to be a little more productive and efficient with their time?' (Duffy, 2014). In many domains, presenting oneself as achieving the ideals of productivity, flexibility, responsiveness to change and entrepreneurialism is a sign of success and superior self-control. The entrepreneurial self who is able to be flexible, high-performing, self-managed and responsive to change is a key figure in workplace culture. Indeed some software has been designed to explicitly combine wellness with productivity objectives (as in the Virgin Pulse program). As such forums suggest, both in workplace culture and in cultures outside of the workplace there is evidence of the blurring of domains. The ideal worker is not only productive in his or her work outputs and achievements; such a worker is healthy, fit and lean. The physically fit and active person is also a productive, successful worker (Kelly, 2013; Longhurst, 2000).

Representations of embodiment

Metaphors of the body that portray it as a machine, and more specifically as a computerised information 'system, are frequently employed in discourses on self-tracking and the quantified self. According to the Wikipedia definition, '[t]he Quantified Self is a movement to incorporate technology into data acquisition on aspects of a person's daily life in terms of inputs (e.g. food consumed, quality of surrounding air), states (e.g. mood, arousal, blood oxygen levels), and performance (mental and physical)' (Quantified Self, 2015d). This definition immediately begins to construct a view of the body/self as a machine-like entity, with 'inputs' and 'outputs' (glossed as 'performance' in the definition) that can readily be measured and quantified.

News reports and blogs similarly tend to use this kind of metaphor when discussing the quantified self. Self-tracking devices, for example, are described as providing 'a dashboard for your body' (*New York Times*, 4 August 2011), and self-trackers are often described as 'body hacking' or as 'bio hackers'. According to the *Guardian* (25 January 2013), '[y]our body isn't a temple, it's a data factory emitting digital exhaust'. Self-trackers are also positioned as scientists who experiment on their own bodies in their own best interests. References are made regularly in news article to quantified selfers as 'body experimenters' and 'their own lab rats' or 'guinea pigs'. Quantifying the self is 'the science of the self', as *Metro Beijing*'s headline puts it (17 December 2012), and it involves people's 'turning their bodies into medical labs' (*Observer* [UK], 25 November 2012). As the American

Newsweek International (10–17 January 2011) describes one self-tracker, such a person is attempting 'to understand the human machine with a dose of science and a whole lot of data crunching'.

At a more symbolic level, self-tracking devices can be understood as the prosthetics of selfhood. For Lury (1997: 3), prosthesis renders self-extension possible, constituting a form of identity in which 'I can, therefore I am' is constructed. We might understand in a similar way the data assemblages that are configured when people use self-tracking devices as prosthetic forms of selfhood and embodiment. There is a doubling of technological prosthetics that occurs in the use of digital technologies for self-tracking. Technological prostheses such as wearable technologies or smartphones and their apps, all of which can be used for self-tracking, in turn generate datalogical prostheses. Embodiment and identity are performed both by engaging with, carrying or wearing a self-tracking device (acts that symbolise a certain type of self: the self-tracking self) and by generating personal data that can be used in certain specific ways as part of the project of selfhood and embodiment.

Early lifeloggers placed a great deal of emphasis on the use of digital technologies to enhance the capacities of human memory. Digitised lifelogging is represented as a form of memory facilitation, drawing on the notion that the internet and computing archives are a form of 'shared external memory' and digital devices, particularly mobile, wearable technologies, facilitate the information collection that contributes to this external memory system (Czerski, 2012). Indeed one of the major motivations for Gordon Bell's MyLifeBits project was his attempt to use digital technologies as a surrogate memory. In an interview, he described his project as giving him 'a kind of a feeling of cleanliness ... I can offload my memory. I feel much freer about remembering something now. I've got this machine, this slave, that does it' (quoted in Thompson, 2006). Some writers on the quantified self have extended the metaphor of the body-machine by portraying self-tracking devices as producing knowledge about the self through technological 'exosenses' that extend the body's sensory capabilities (Swan, 2012b, 2012a, 2013).

This vision of the body as augmented by self-tracking devices presents a concept in which such devices not only become its prosthetics but extend it into a network of other bodies and objects. Adopting the concept of code/space, we can think about the interactions and intersections of self-trackers with their digital devices as bringing software together with the materiality not only of the objects that self-trackers use in order to monitor themselves and have their data displayed, but of the data themselves. There are various ways in which self-tracking devices can be understood as prosthetics. Such devices, when attached to or worn on or inside the body, become physical extensions of it. They extend the capabilities and spatial dimensions of embodiment. Given the intensified integration of our bodies and selves with our digital technologies, many of us have become so thoroughly a digitised assemblage that this mode of being is now taken for granted.

As digital technologies have transmuted into digital forms, particularly into smaller and more easily wearable forms, it becomes less obvious where the body ends and the technology begins. This is most overtly the case of such technologies as heart pacemakers, insulin pumps and cochlear implants, all of which are inserted into the body in unobtrusive ways. But this loss of boundary between body and gadget is also – and increasingly – an element in all the types of digital technologies that we use for self-tracking bodily functions and activities: smartphones, armbands, clothing or watches embedded with sensors. In terms of nonwearable sensors, when the environments in which we occupy space – be they our beds, our homes, our cars or public spaces – are embedded with sensors, our bodies become incorporated into these places, interact with them and come to be the subjects of these sensors. We may carry our sensors on us, but we also enter into sensor-equipped places that automatically start to generate data in response to us. We become incorporated into these code/spaces for the time we are occupying them.

Techno-utopian representations of the possibilities of self-tracking devices and the data they are able to generate have been very common in popular culture, particularly in early portrayals of self-tracking and the quantified self. Using digital self-tracking technologies, humans are represented as becoming yet one more node in the Internet of Things, exchanging data not only with other humans but also with objects and material environments (Swan, 2012b). The body in this discourse is positioned as a 'smart machine' interlinked to other 'smart machines'. Bodily sensations become phenomena that are mediated and augmented through machines, transformed into data and then communicated back to the human user.

The affective dimensions of self-tracking

Extending the idea of evocative objects to self-tracking devices and to the information and visualisations they generate, we can view these devices as material objects that are invested with highly personal meaning and emotion. This is relevant not only to the physical objects that people handle as part of their self-tracking practices (pen and paper, diaries, cameras, wearables, smartphones and so on), but also to the computer software and platforms that are used as part of digitised self-monitoring. Software stores personal data and is itself altered by people's interactions with them because of the responsiveness of their algorithms. The customisation of Google tools such as Google Search and Google Now and the recommendations made by such platforms as Amazon are examples of the ways in which software responds to users. The personal data that are collected using self-tracking devices – photographs, videos, messages, interactions on social media, calendar entries, geolocation information, bodily functions and activities – become a biographical repository of significance and meaning to the user. They are 'my data'.

As people engage with the objects they use for self-tracking, the objects themselves become transformed through customisation and personalisation. The devices that are used for self-tracking are responsive to and potentially alter our bodies, but our bodies also react to and transform the devices. Pens leave marks on paper; wearables and smartphones begin to archive the unique personal details of their users' lives, and their physical surfaces are marked by the bodies of their users – their sweat, body oils, fingerprints and so on. Indeed some self-tracking devices are worn inside the body, being encased by and interacting with internal bodily organs, fluids and tissues – for example the digital tablets that are swallowed, the pelvic floor-monitoring devices that are inserted into the vaginal cavity and the continuous glucose monitors that are inserted under the skin on the user's stomach.

Self-tracking devices are therefore biographical and personal in several ways: they collect and record data about one's life; they archive these data; and they themselves become transformed and personalised, marked by the user's body and behaviours in unique ways, as part of a process of appropriation and domestication. In this sense, contemporary self-tracking tools and records are the latter-day versions of the paper diary or journal, photo album, keepsake and memento box or personal dossier. Indeed, as the personal digital data that people generate via self-tracking are algorithmically manipulated and represented in certain forms, they become part of the performance of algorithmic selfhood, in which using digital platforms and personal data may strategically become a mode of self-promotion (Pasquale, 2015).

Newer self-tracking devices have been designed to facilitate and engage the wearer's emotional responses and intimate relationships. As we have seen in Chapter 1, according to Tim Cook the Apple Watch is 'the most personal device' ever created by Apple (Colt, 2014). Such products rely on haptics – tactile feedback technologies that involve interacting with a user's body by touching it on the inside or on the outside. The Apple Watch not only monitors the haptic functions and signs of the wearer's body, it also communicates with the wearer and others whom the wearer includes in her or his use, and it does so by employing physical sensations. Apple refers to the technology contained in the Watch as a 'taptic engine', which uses haptic technology to 'tap' users on the wrist to alert them to a notification on the Watch. The blurb on the Apple website contends that, 'since Apple Watch sits on your wrist, your alerts aren't just immediate. They're intimate ... We found a way to give technology a more human touch. Literally.' Users can also send 'taps' to other Watch users, to alert them to a message they wish them to see, or even to share the sensation of their heartbeats (Apple, 2014).

People may respond emotionally to the data that are generated about themselves through self-tracking technologies.

Many social media platforms automatically track the popularity of their users. Once users engage in these platforms, both voluntary and involuntary self-tracking operates, as it is impossible for users not to be confronted with information about how others have responded to their content. While many people may wish to see the numbers of followers or friends they have on these platforms, or how often their status update has been 'liked', 'favoured' or retweeted, others may not consider these numbers important or may find them confrontational, if they regard such numbers as indicators of personal worth, popularity, impact, influence or social standing (Bucher, 2012; Gerlitz and Helmond, 2013). So, too, the information that self-tracking apps and other software feed back to people on their bodily functions or activities, their moods, their financial status or their work productivity may elicit a wide range of emotions, from pleasure and a sense of satisfaction to disappointment, frustration, or even anger.

Emotional responses are also imbricated in the ways in which people who choose to self-track or not are conceptualised. Underlying many accounts of self-tracking is a barely hidden discourse of morality, which takes the form of championing those who take action to improve themselves. When one adopts this kind of rationale for entrepreneurial self-optimisation and for the search for self-knowledge as a means to achieve it, one makes the implicit assumption that those people who choose not to engage in practices of selfhood or fail to engage successfully in them are in some way deficient: ignorant, lacking the appropriate drive, or wilfully self-neglecting. This is perhaps most evident in the ways in which self-tracking practices have been taken up in the medical and public health domains, where individual self-management and an emphasis on personal responsibility for taking steps to prevent disease and early death have long featured (Brandt and Rozin, 1997; Lupton, 1995b, 2013b; Petersen and Lupton, 1996). When a growing panoply of technological devices for gathering information about one's body becomes available and people use it to engage in optimising the body/self, then a moral imperative to do so emerges. And when notions of health, wellbeing and productivity are generated via data drawn from self-monitoring, the social determinants of these attributes are covered over. Illness, emotional distress, lack of happiness or lack of productivity in the workplace come to be represented primarily as failures of self-control or efficiency on the part of individuals, and therefore as requiring greater or more effective individual efforts – including perhaps self-tracking regimens of increased intensity – to produce a 'better self'.

Intentions to self-track, however, are not always supported by the affordances of the technologies themselves. An important element of sociomaterial studies is the acknowledgement that the assemblages that come together when humans and nonhumans interact are fragile and open to change. Because they are made up of many different actors, changes, failures and adjustments are inevitable (Albrechtslund and Lauritsen, 2013). In the case of self-tracking technologies, as the research reviewed in Chapter 1 suggested, devices may not work as expected by either their developers or their users. They may break down, fail to synchronise with other devices as they should, or lose their power or their internet connection. People may hack their device, using it in ways that were not planned by the manufacturers; or they may forget to wear it; or they may drop and damage it. Indeed many self-trackers express frustration at what they perceive to be the lack of functionality of their monitoring devices: the devices' failure to work as the users think they should. Alternatively, some self-trackers may become almost unreasonably disappointed when they realise that they have not worn or activated their device when attempting to self-track.

Some people find wearable self-tracking devices not fashionable enough, or not waterproof enough, or too clunky or heavy, or not comfortable enough to wear; or they find that these devices get destroyed in the washing machine when the user forgets to remove them from his or her clothing. Ruckenstein's (2014) interviews with Finnish users of heart-rate and physical activity digital monitors found that some remarked on their awareness of the devices. As one woman commented: 'Last night, I noticed that the measuring equipment suddenly started physically annoying me quite a lot. I would have liked to have ripped if off, even if just for the night' (2014: 75).

Designer Jennifer Darmour (2013) has argued that the aesthetic dimension of wearable technologies has been little addressed. If these technologies remain too obvious, she argues, 'bolting' devices to our bodies (an unlikely Franken-stein metaphor) and therefore obviously proclaiming our-selves cyborgs will 'distract, disrupt, and ultimately disengage us from others, ultimately degrading our human experience' (ibid.). Darmour asserts that these objects need to be designed more carefully, so that they may be 'seamlessly' integrated into the 'fabric of our lives' (ibid.). Her suggested ways of doing this include making self-tracking devices look more beautiful, like jewellery (brooches, necklaces, bracelets, rings), incorporating them into fashionable garments, making them peripheral, making them meaningful, and using colours or vibrations rather than numbers to display data readings from them.

On her blog, Carol Torgan (2012), a health strategist and educator, has remarked upon the emotions that wearing digital self-tracking devices may provoke in people. She notes that putting on a self-tracking device makes some people feel athletic, others fashionable, still others fat and self-conscious about their bodies. Others feel safer and develop a greater sense of security about having their health monitored by these devices. Torgan also emphasises that the design of the device – its 'look', its conspicuousness or lack thereof – may be integral to how people feel when they wear it. Design fea-tures, emotions, bodies, selves and data are entangled in the digitised self-tracking experience.

Taking and losing control

A further element of the emotional dimensions of self-tracking relates to concepts of taking or losing control. The idealised reflexive monitoring subject, as represented in popular forums and in some of the academic literature that focuses on the benefits of self-tracking, is highly rational, motivated and data-centric. Underpinning this ideal is the belief that the self-knowledge that eventuates will allow self-trackers to exert greater control over their destinies than they had before. Sociologists' writings on these topics suggest that self-tracking might be understood, at least partly, as people's response to the problem of dealing with the uncertainties and openness of choice of late modernity. One aspect of this ideal of the responsible, entrepreneurial self is the imperative nature of actively avoiding risk and of attempting to monitor and manage one's health as part of promoting one's life chances. In a world in which risks and threats appear to be ever present, the certainties promised by the intense monitoring of the self-tracker may be interpreted as a means of containing risk and controlling the vagaries of fate to some extent. The data derived from self-tracking appear to offer at least some degree of certainty, which one's own perceptions cannot attain, and a relatively high degree of control over the messiness and unpredictability of the fleshly body.

In matters of health, self-tracking offers users of such technologies a strategy by which they feel as if they could gather data from their health indicators as a means of avoiding illness and disease. As a news article on the quantified self has it, practices like self-tracking puts people 'in charge of their health' (*Daily Star* [Lebanon], 22 April 2010). This notion of control, of taking charge of one's body, is an important attraction for many of those who self-track. The research studies about self-tracking practices that I reviewed in Chapter 1 – as well as self-trackers' own accounts in blog posts or in the Quantified Self website's show-and-tell presentations that self-trackers use to describe how they track and what they gain from it – suggest that there are many benefits and consolations to those who engage in these practices. People commonly talk about achieving a sense of control over their lives, particularly over those elements that previously seemed chaotic or challenging: a chronic illness, body weight, stress, sleeping problems, moods, relationships, medical treatments, physical fitness, hormonal fluctuations, reproductive cycles, mental concentration and so on. Some self-trackers find that sharing their data with a small group of intimate others helps their relationships and garners support for the changes they are attempting to make. Others discuss becoming more aware of aspects of their lives such as their embodiment, social relationships and emotions – or simply enjoying creating new forms of information about themselves and discovering patterns in their everyday lives.

Concepts of 'patient engagement' now frequently include reference to self-monitoring and self-care – or even quantified-self – practices, often carried out with the help of digitised devices. I use the phrase 'digitally engaged patient' to describe this ideal (Lupton, 2013a). Other commentators have more specifically employed the phrase 'quantified patient', drawing on quantified self discourses. Thus, for example, an editorial published by a group of doctors in the journal *Current Medical Research and Opinion* makes direct reference to the Quantified Self movement by championing the idea of what the authors call 'a patient participatory culture' – which they believe can be supported through practices associated with the 'quantified patient' concept. In that editorial self-tracking practices are represented as allowing patients to become more engaged in their healthcare by conducting their own self-monitoring and by sharing their data with their healthcare providers (Appelboom, LoPresti, Reginster, Sander Connolly, and Dumont, 2014).

The ideal 'quantified patient' takes up the opportunities afforded by digital self-tracking devices to manage his or her chronic illness or prevent disease (Swan, 2012a). Eric Topol, one of the most ardent advocates of using digital health technologies, including self-tracking devices, for patient engagement, argues that patients can and should become experts on themselves with the help of these technologies. He asserts that this will radically alter the doctor–patient relationship, shifting the balance of power from doctors as medical experts to patients as more knowledgeable than ever about their own bodies thanks to the affordances of digital technologies that allow them to generate personal health information. 'Smart patients' are configured by their interactions with their smart devices (Topol, 2015). Writers in the preventive medicine and health-promotion literatures have also begun to refer to the importance of self-tracking bodily activities as a way of preventing disease that is believed to be self-imposed. Many draw on the persuasive computing model to contend that lay people need to be nudged or encouraged in order to take up self-tracking devices as part of individual health-promotion efforts (Purpura, Schwanda, Williams, Stubler, and Sengers, 2011; Rooksby, Rost, Morrison, and Chalmers, 2014).

One success story is that recounted on his blog by Dan Hon (2012). Hon has type 2 diabetes and uses the Nike Fuelband and Fitbit wearable devices to monitor his physical activity levels as well as a digital blood glucose meter and weight scales. He reported that the combination of these technologies had allowed him to reduce his blood sugar levels to normal and that he had 'healed myself through data' (Hon, 2012). In a post published on the Quantified Self website, self-tracker Seth Roberts (2012) noted that his reflexive self-monitoring has led to better sleep, weight loss, a better mood, reduction of inflammation in his body, fewer colds, better balance, a better functioning brain and improved blood sugar levels. Roberts claimed that he had even managed to improve his acne skin condition by experimenting with various treatments and was thereby able to identify which treatments worked well for him, achieving greater knowledge than his dermatologist was able to display. He wrote that both the information he had gathered on himself and his engagement in self-tracking had 'made me believe I had more power over my health than I thought' (Roberts, 2012).

For some self-trackers, the ideal consists of technologies and sensor-equipped environments that automatically sense and collect data on users' lives without requiring direct intervention from users. Blumtritt (2014), for example, has expressed his contemplations on the future of the quantified self thus: 'Data will become integral with our sensory, biological self. And as we get more and more connected, our feeling of being tied into one body will also fade, as we become data creatures, bodiless, angelized.' Such a perspective harkens back to the speculative futures of the cyborg body in cyberspace, in which the 'meat' of the body was represented as ideally left behind when the person entered virtual reality (Lupton, 1995a). Yet, in its intense focus on collecting detailed information about the body and behaviours, self-tracking is far from being a disembodied experience. The assemblage that is configured by self-tracking technologies supports a reflexive, self-monitoring awareness of the body, bringing the body to the fore in ways that challenge the idea of a nonreflexive, absent body (Leder, 1990). The body is hardly able to disappear when its functions, movements and habits are constantly monitored and the user is made continually made aware of these dispositions.

People may also feel ambivalent about self-tracking itself as a practice. As discussed in Chapter 1, for some people self-tracking may be a sign of weakness, of inability to engage in self-management without technological assistance. Others find that they become too obsessive about self-tracking, losing sight of other aspects of their lives. The intense focus on the body that these devices encourage may place too much pressure on oneself, causing feelings of failure and self-hatred. Some people who were enthusiastic self-trackers have written accounts of eventually relinquishing collecting personal data, or at least scaling back on their efforts.

One formerly ardent member of the Quantified Self movement, Alexandra Carmichael (2010), published a poem on the Quantified Self website in which she described how, '[a]fter 40 measurements a day for 1.5 years', she stopped self-tracking. She describes the self-punishment, fear and hatred 'behind the tracking' and observes: 'I had stopped trusting myself. Letting the numbers drown out. My intuition. My instincts.' Carmichael goes on to recount how she was concerned that she had become 'addicted' to using her devices to self-track and was 'beating myself up' if her data suggested that she was lazy and out of control of her body. For Carmichael, her data revealed a lack of ability to self-regulate and caused her to feel as if she were punishing herself.

Dan Hon was initially pleased with how his diabetes had been controlled through self-tracking, with the help of a plethora of digital tools. Some months later, however, he began to reconsider this positive assessment when he realised the effect his 'numbers' could have on his state of mind and mood:

> From a mental health point of view, one of the things that I realised about myself was that I was only really happy when numbers were trending in the right direction. When blood sugar and weight were coming down, that was great. But the wearable systems that we have at the moment aren't particularly good (and obviously that depends on how you define 'good') for what happens when the numbers are trending in the wrong direction. (Hon, 2014)

One of the most interesting accounts of self-tracking via digital devices is a conference paper giving an autoethnographic account by Kaiton Williams, a technologist and a designer. Williams begins with the sentence: 'One year and 617,496 calories ago, I decided that I needed to get back in touch with my self and back in control of my body' (Williams, 2013). He goes on to comment that he found that self-tracking through smartphone apps was effective at making him achieve his goals of managing his diet, losing weight and engaging in regular exercise. However, while he lost weight, he found that nonweight-related aspects of his life began to be reinterpreted through the lens of these devices. Williams notes that he began to trust the digital data over his own physical sensations, and that the data also began to shape how he felt:

> We (the Apps and I) had co-constructed a digital model of my self, and here I was, managing myself, it seems, by proxy. The feedback from that digital model often took precedence over how I physically felt. When I didn't eat 'enough' protein I felt weaker, and when I had too much sugar I felt fatter. These were delayed reactions; a re-reading of my body from the model. I've yet to decide: is this model pushing me closer in contact or further away from my self and my world? (Williams, 2013)

Williams discusses how rendering his life more calculable via tracking apps changed his eating habits so that they fit the technical requirements of the apps. 'I prioritized certain foods and recipes, and avoided others to work best within the capabilities of the food database' (2013). Instead of the pleasure of eating or preparing food, Williams found that he was focusing on how better to shape his eating practices to suit the apps.

As Williams' account suggests, some aspects of every life and sensual experience become lost or ignored when the focus is directed on what a self-tracking device is able to measure or what it might reveal. This was also evident in Craig Mod's experience of visiting Paris. He used his Fitbit to count his steps as he walked around this celebrated city. Mod found himself choosing places to visit and routes on the basis of how many steps he could accumulate on his device that day. When Mod discovered that he had forgotten to wear his Fitbit one day, he was initially devastated that his steps around Paris had not been counted: 'Part of me wanted to cab it back to the hotel. Cab it back and clip on the Fitbit and do the walk again. All of it. Mirrored and remapped. Climb the Eiffel steps once more. Ground it. Make it real in the ether.' But then he realised that he was better able to enjoy the beauty of the city without the distraction of monitoring his steps (Mod, 2012).

The anonymous author of the blog 'The Unquantified Self' writes about her use of counting for the purpose of gaining control when she is feeling under particular stress and life appears to have moved out of control. She describes how she became 'a card-carrying member of the Quantified Self movement'. This woman used self-tracking devices and apps to document her life in ever finer detail. Her blog outlines the reasons why she decided to attempt to give up self-tracking; these reasons include wasting too much time on the practices, becoming too judgemental of others and of herself (even in the form of inciting guilt and self-recrimination), and discovering that her data simply revealed the 'bleeding obvious'. Her sense of control was lost as she found herself becoming obsessive about self-tracking and losing control in a different way. Then she found it difficult when pressures in her life became intense once more, and she took up self-tracking again to deal with them: 'I just had to start tracking and counting steps again. I know it's crazy and makes no sense. Just that feeling that my life could go out of control made me reach for the comfort of my numbers' (Anonymous, 2014).

An interesting discussion took place in the comments section of a blog called 'Your Eatopia', which is directed at providing support for people who are attempting to recover from restrictive eating disorders – that is, harmful ways of reducing one's food intake, as in eating disorders or in continual and obsessive dieting that stems from anxiety – or from compulsive overexercising. The blog's author expressed her concern that people engaging in restrictive eating may find their behaviours exacerbated through the use of self-tracking devices and that this development contributes to anxiety and hypervigilance about diet and body weight (Olwyn, 2015). One commentator on her blog noted that she was using a pedometer in the attempt to ensure that she did not engage in too much exercise (as people with restrictive eating

disorders often also exercise compulsively), but was concerned that checking her steps could become yet another
compulsion. Another woman noted in a comment that she
was encouraged by her employer to engage in self-tracking
in order to reduce her health insurance premiums:

> I opted to pay the higher health insurance premium in order
> to avoid being told what my numbers should be and how I
> supposedly need to eat, breath[e], sleep, think, excrete and
> move according to their flawed guidelines. It seems like
> another way to send the message that we as humans aren't
> good enough and need guidance to just be ok. I find it wrong
> on so many levels.

In such accounts there is evidence of ambivalence about,
and even rejection of, the sense of control that self-tracking
may give people. On the one hand, reflexive self-monitoring
can provide reassurance, a feeling of exerting order over the
chaos of a person's body or life, an enhanced sense of
self-knowledge and self-management as one conforms to the
ideal of the well-regulated citizen. The 'comfort of numbers'
can be enticing. On the other hand, self-tracking can begin
to make people feel as if they were losing control when it
descends into an obsession, compulsion or 'addiction' with
one's data to the exclusion of other aspects of one's life
and when the data begin to make one feel dissatisfied or
inadequate.

Selfhood and surveillance

The opportunity to share one's data with others on social
networking sites also incorporates the 'wisdom of the crowd'
into the self-help expert apparatus. Friends and followers or
other users of the app or platform can become experts,
drawing on their own experiences to comment on other users'
progress and to give constructive advice, and vice versa.
Aggregated personal data in the form of big data offer another
form of crowd-sourced expertise for the digitised self-help
apparatus. Thus, for example, patient support platforms
such as PatientsLikeMe create opportunities for people with
specific conditions not only to track their treatments and

symptoms, but to share these details with others and to contribute to a developing database that provides similar patients with the insights offered by the combined personal data of members.

As I explained in Chapter 2, there are various modes of surveillance that operate when people use digital technologies. Whether or not digital technologies are used, self-tracking that is undertaken for purely personal and private purposes can be interpreted as voluntary self-surveillance (Albrechtslund and Lauritsen, 2013; Best, 2010). The use of digital self-tracking technologies blurs the spatial boundaries between public and private surveillance, bringing public surveillance into the domestic sphere but also often extending private surveillance out into public domains. The practice of reflexive self-tracking constructs users as personally responsible for their own care and self-management, but also as part of a heterogeneous network of actors, which includes the various technologies employed as well as friends and contacts. Various forms of self-tracking assemblages are brought into being as these networks of humans and nonhumans, flesh and technology come into contact with one another and intertwine.

Notions of privacy are challenged and transformed by the interplay of often very personal information about the individual that is generated via self-tracking and the movement of this information into social media sites, into dedicated self-tracking platforms, or simply into the archives of the computing cloud, where it becomes open to access and can be seen by others. The opportunity to generate personal data from one's interactions on social media sites and to share these or other data with others on these sites is a new way of engaging in voluntary self-watching. Here self-trackers can offer their personal data to others and view the data of others, both these actions being acts of sousveillance. Here self-surveillance moves from an inner-directed preoccupation with the body/self to a performative mode, inviting further scrutiny from one's friends and followers. Not only do platforms such as Facebook and Twitter generate data that can be used for self-tracking, they allow people to share personal information with hundreds or more of their friends or followers – and this information includes regular automated updates on people's exercise and dietary habits or body weight. Friends and followers are invited by the user to contribute to monitoring his or her bodily habits: the net of surveillance is thus expanded around the user's body and practices of selfhood. When self-tracking practices involve collecting and recording information on other people (when, for example, an automated camera worn around one's neck takes photographic images throughout the day, including images of other people), then they may also involve sousveillance, either carried out deliberately or emerging as a unintended outcome of using these technologies.

Whitson (2013) has noted the gamification aspects of contemporary digital self-tracking, which are a part of voluntary surveillance practices. She explores issues around the self-surveillance and the invitation of surveillance from others that gamification involves. As Whitson contends, engaging in self-surveillance may be experienced as ludic in its own right, quite apart from any other aspect that may involve game-like elements – such as competition with others or the use of a storyline that involves taking on a character and engaging in quests. Quite simply, it can be fun to generate numbers about oneself and to challenge oneself to achieve goals. When an act of surveillance is rendered playful and wilful or consenting, it becomes far more acceptable than those acts of surveillance that are perceived as being imposed by others. This perspective is evident in the words of self-tracking cyclist Andrea Parrish, who has written that she enjoys tracking her rides and her weight and calorie input and output because she views these activities as playful, and thus they enhance her motivation: 'Tracking what I am doing and the effects those actions have appeals to the data-loving, game-making, goal-oriented part of my brain. Tracking keeps me accountable to myself and allows me to turn what might otherwise be a chore into a challenge' (Parrish, 2012).

The sense of intimacy and social support that many self-trackers derive from using social media to share their personal data may readily translate into uploading information about their bodies through self-tracking devices. Such information may be regarded as contributing to the persona that is constructed via social media sites: sharing attempts to reduce smoking or drinking, or to engage regularly in exercise, for example, and receiving supportive messages in response, as well as commiseration for those times when the user fails to achieve her or his goals of self-improvement and discipline. However, some users may still feel uncomfortable about what they perceive as exposure and invasion of their personal space. They may also feel 'invaded' by the sheer overload of data that membership of social networking sites may generate and by the difficulty of switching off mobile devices and taking time out from using them (boyd, 2008).

As self-tracking has spread from purely voluntary and private reasons to other rationales, other forms of veillance are involved. Traditional external, top-down surveillance is implicated when people are pushed or coerced into engaging in self-tracking or into giving up their personal data to others for the latter's own purposes. Self-tracking digital technologies may be viewed in some instances as operating so as to facilitate panoptic surveillance. When, for example, school children in physical education classes are required to wear digital heart-rate monitors, they must conform to the set exercise schedule and review the tracking data that the monitor generates, because they are never quite sure when their teacher is checking their data. Similarly, workers who have signed up to a corporate wellness program involving the use of fitness trackers and who know that their participation may augur well with their supervisors, or that by participating they are conforming to the dominant workplace culture of self-tracked fitness, become implicated in a panoptic mode of surveillance. In both instances the initial impetus comes from another actor, as part of encouraged self-tracking. Participants in these forms of self-tracking may feel that these practices are imposed on them and that they have little choice about participating. For some, however, the motivation to continue to engage in reflexive self-monitoring may become internalised and experienced as the result of a voluntary decision that conforms to their personal objectives.

There are also political issues to consider when discussing how the personal data that individuals generate regarding themselves are used for other, surveillance purposes. The use and ownership of personal data by actors and agencies other than the individual who generates these data are beginning to have major implications for social discrimination and justice issues. Again, the use of personal data by others may take place without people's having any control or even knowledge of how the data are analysed and employed. Rather than reflexive self-monitoring acting as an avenue of autonomy and optimisation of one's life, the information it generates may be used to close off opportunities and freedoms (see further discussion of this problem in Chapter 5).

In this chapter I have addressed the ways in which self-tracking cultures are underpinned by contemporary concepts and discourses related to selfhood and the body. The next chapter moves on to examining the ways in which forms of information about the self and the body are conceptualised and acted upon. Self-tracking is, above all, a type of gathering and making sense of personal information, and ideas and discourses about numbers, quantification and data are major contributors to reflexive self-monitoring practices.

4

'You Are Your Data'

Personal Data Meanings, Practices and Materialisations

I have made various references in this book thus far to the importance that is placed on gathering and acting on information about oneself in self-tracking cultures. Self-tracking involves making many decisions about what information to collect and how to represent it, make sense of it and apply it. This chapter explores in greater detail the concepts of data and the strategies of the data practices and data materialisations that characterise contemporary self-tracking cultures.

The meaning and value of personal digital data

Self-tracking activities that use digital technologies are one type of prosumption, generating as they do highly personal information about users who may record many details about their bodies, daily activities, social encounters and relationships. Like many other forms of digital data, self-tracking data have a vitality and a social life of their own, circulating across and between a multitude of sites. In a context in which digital data are culturally represented as liquid entities that require management and containment, part of the project of managing the contemporary body/self is one of containment

of the data that are generated about oneself. Therefore the
discourse of control in discussions about self-tracking is often
not only about controlling one's body and one's self by using
data (as I suggested in Chapter 3), but exerting control over
the data themselves. As discursive representations of self-
tracking and the quantified self frequently contend, personal
data are profligate. One should seek first to collect these data
and, second, to manage and discipline them by aggregating
them, by representing them visually, and by making sense
of them.

The diversity of approaches to self-tracking results in a
range of data sets being established on the body and on the
self. Shifting forms of selfhood are configured via personal
data assemblages, depending on the context in which and
purpose for which they are assembled. As the digital data
produced through self-tracking are constantly generated and
the combinations of data sets that may be brought together
on individuals are numerous, personal data assemblages are
never stable or contained. With the help of self-tracking
devices, the body and the self are enacted and reconfigured
throughout the process. The Fitbit physical activity-tracking
device produces some forms of data that may or may not be
acted on by the user, as does the productivity app or the mood
tracker, for example. Each configures a different and constantly changing data assemblage around the user, and these
assemblages may intersect or not, as the user deems appropriate. Data assemblages are constantly open to reconfiguration,
and hence reinterpretation. They are also recursive and reflexive. Self-trackers may take note of the information that is
generated about themselves and change their behaviour
accordingly, which then may change the data outputs – and
so on. Some forms of data assemblages may be used on some
occasions and others ignored or discounted.

When a personal data assemblage is generated, it represents a 'snapshot' of a particular moment in time and of a
particular rationale for data practice; or, to use a different
metaphor, a data assemblage configures data that are 'frozen',
their liquidity rendered solid. As I discussed in Chapter 2,
bodies and selves are always multiple, in whatever context
they find themselves. However, for self-trackers, this multiplicity is foregrounded in ways that may not have occurred

in previous eras. If self-trackers are reviewing their personal data regularly, they cannot fail to be confronted with the shifting data assemblages that serve to represent their bodies and their selves. Some of the data practices in which they are invited to engage as part of self-tracking culture consist therefore of negotiation and sense making around the hybridity and vitality of their data assemblages.

Self-trackers or third parties who seek to use their data must engage in sense making that can gain some purchase on their mutating forms. Indeed the aim of the Quantified Self movement, as its inventors Gary Wolf and Kevin Kelly suggest on their website, 'is to help people get meaning out of their personal data' (Quantified Self, 2015a). Many participants in the Quantified Self movement engage in reflexive practices concerning which data to collect and why, what they plan to do with their data, how they can improve their methods, how it feels to collect and use data and what the wider implications are for their concepts of selfhood and embodiment. As Wolf (2013) puts it in a comment on one of the Quantified Self website's forums: 'Our role is not to "sell" this technology to ourselves, but to use it thoughtfully and share our knowledge, so that we add reflective capacity – that is, some thoughtfulness – to the systems we and others are making.'

'Data' is a keyword in discourses on self-tracking – as in 'the data-driven lifestyle', a phrase that was used as the headline for an article by Gary Wolf for his *New York Times* magazine article in 2010 (Wolf, 2010). In an earlier article that appeared in the *Washington Post*, Wolf was quoted as commenting: 'For a certain type of person, data is [*sic*] the most important thing you can trust. Certain people think a feeling of inner certainty is misleading' (quoted in Hesse, 2008). A self-tracker interviewed for this article agreed with this sentiment: 'I want to understand the changes that are actually happening [in my life], not just my perceptions of them.' The author of this news story goes on to assert: 'Computers don't lie. People lie.' The other co-founder of the Quantified Self movement, Kevin Kelly, makes reference to the importance of data in a blog post in which he argues that everyone will begin to self-track, because '[a]lmost everything we do today generates data' and, as a result, 'today capturing data about ourselves is often trivially easy ... Because tracking our data is so easy, more and more folks are doing it.' Kelly asserts that, because so large a volume of data is created on individuals, learning how to interpret and use these data has become an important life skill and will become 'the new normal' (Kelly, 2011).

Wolf went on to expand on his ideas about the vagaries of fleshly perception in his *New York Times* article. He began with a description of the error-prone judgement of humans and their inability to remember details and patterns from their everyday lives. As a consequence, Wolf contends: 'We make decisions with partial information. We are forced to steer by guesswork. We go with our gut' (Wolf, 2010). He asserts that, '[i]f you want to replace the vagaries of intuition with something more reliable, you first need to gather data. Once you know the facts, you can live by them.' Duncan Watts, social scientist at Microsoft Research, has also argued for the importance of collecting personal data; and he has done so by contrasting instinct, tradition and received wisdom with the more reliable evidence provided by self-tracking data: 'If you had to choose between a world in which you do everything based on instinct, tradition or some vague, received wisdom, or you do something based on evidence, I would say the latter is the way to go' (quoted in Feiler, 2014).

Wired magazine has played a major role in introducing concepts of self-tracking to its readership. In the same issue that hosted Wolf's initial piece outlining his vision of the quantified self (Wolf, 2009, to which I referred in Chapter 1), *Wired* published four other articles on quantified self-tracking, each focusing on a specific area: running, exercise in general, health and nutrition. One of these was entitled 'The Nike experiment: How the shoe giant unleashed the power of personal metrics' (McClusky, 2009). The article described the experiences of people who were using what was then a new technology: Nike+, the wearable sensor device and associated platform for monitoring physical activity. One woman interviewed for the article described herself as a 'stat whore' who found these quantified data highly motivating. 'She attributes much of her newfound fitness to the power of data ... "I can log into Nike+ and see what I've done over the past year," she says. "That's really powerful for me ... I don't have to question what I've done. The data is [*sic*] right there in white and green"' (quoted in McClusky, 2009).

According to the author of this article, digital quantified self-tracking performed via devices such as Nike+ offers a means of obtaining data that shed light on the workings of the body and of the self. The body/self is portrayed as a conglomerate of quantifiable data that can be revealed by using digital devices:

> We tend to think of our physical selves as a system that's simply too complex to comprehend. But what we've learned from companies like Google is that if you can collect enough data, there's no need for a grand theory to explain a phenomenon. You can observe it all through the numbers. Everything is data. *You* are your data, and once you understand that data, you can act on it [*sic*]. (McClusky, 2009)

It is argued that such analysis leads to greater efficiency and productivity, as suggested by the phrases 'personal analytics' and 'personal informatics'. Stephen Wolfram, a complexity theorist and the CEO (chief executive officer) of a software company, claims to have coined the expression 'personal analytics' on the basis of the following reasoning: 'There's organizational analytics, which is looking at an organization and trying to understand what the data says [*sic*] about its operation. Personal analytics is what you can figure out applying analytics to the person, to understand the operation of the person' (quoted in Regalado, 2013). The language of such descriptions often mimics that of organisational, managerial or computing rhetoric, as in this statement from an article on the possibilities of reflexive self-monitoring, which is written by a futurist: 'The long-term vision of QS activity is that of a systemic monitoring approach where an individual's continuous personal information climate provides real-time performance optimization suggestions' (Swan, 2013: 85).

It has been argued by some commentators that the emergence of new digital technologies for monitoring and measuring human bodies that can easily be used by any individual has led to a democratisation of scientific biological research. The ability to gather, visualise and represent information on human bodies is now no longer confined to the realms of experts in science or medicine (Pantzar and Ruckenstein, 2015). Some self-trackers engage in highly systematic observations of their personal data, attempting to identify correlations between various activities or behaviours and physiological functions or productivity. Not only do these self-trackers make choices concerning the data about themselves that are important to collect; they make sense of and use data in highly specific and individualised ways. They seek to make connections between diverse sets of data: how diet, meditation or caffeine affect their concentration, for example, or how their mood is influenced by exercise, sleep patterns or geographical location, or what the specific interactions of all of these variables are. Indeed the very idiosyncrasy or uniqueness of many self-trackers' interests and consequent data practices means that their data may not be as interesting or valuable to others as they are to the self-trackers themselves (Nafus and Sherman, 2014).

Many portrayals of the information that can be collected about oneself via self-tracking represent such information as offering unprecedented insights. The apparent details that especially digitised self-tracking technologies can provide and their continuous generation are viewed as particularly valuable to reflexive self-monitoring efforts. In his *New York Times* article, Wolf (2010) also points to the difference that sensor-based and other digitised technologies can make to acquiring self-knowledge through numbers: 'Automated sensors do more than give us facts; they also remind us that our ordinary behavior contains obscure quantitative signals that can be used to inform our behavior, once we learn to read them.' This notion that digital self-tracking devices render visible elements of one's self that are not otherwise perceptible has been expressed elsewhere. For example in the *Newshour* report (The quantified self: Data gone wild? 2013) to which I referred in the previous chapter, self-tracker Bob Troia notes: 'I can look down at my phone at any point in the day and see, kind of, how stressed I am.' The implication of this statement is that without his stress-tracking app and the quantification of bodily signs that are deemed to denote the 'stress' experienced by his body, Troia would have no idea of how stressed he is feeling. The technology provides insights that the bodily sensations felt by Troia do not: it interprets these sensations for him. Similarly, in the same report, David Pogue discusses the awareness that may be gained from self-tracking 'into previously invisible aspects of your life'.

As I pointed out in Chapter 3, many references to self-tracking in the popular media represent trackers as scientists ('body hackers') working on their bodies as research tools. The body is represented as a machine that generates data requiring scientific modes of analysis and contains imperceptible flows and ebbs of data that need to be identified, captured and harnessed so that they may be made visible to the observer. In self-tracking cultures, the knowledge of the body that is acquired through the senses requires translation and rendering into recordable information by digital or other devices. Furthermore, these accounts suggest, there are many types of data about our bodies and our selves that we cannot access unless digitised technologies and numerical data are employed. They remain 'invisible' to us until they are collected and rendered into some form of observable information. While the human body may be represented as a computerised information system, in these types of discussions such a system is flawed by comparison with literal computerised technologies. The human computer, in its inevitably fleshly humanness, can never achieve the capabilities offered by real digitised technologies.

The discourse of trusting the data over embodied knowledge, the machine over the human, is evident in these accounts. The data appeared to offer certainty, while the body's perceptions are represented as untrustworthy, inexact, inaccurately mediated through human experience rather than being objective. In these representations, technology and the data it produces are portrayed as offering unique insights into the workings of the human body that individuals' unmediated haptic sensations cannot. Like other biometric technologies, self-tracking devices are viewed as able to peer inside the body, releasing its secrets. These self-tracking discourses therefore fit into a broader understanding of the body, which has been articulated in medicine since the development of visualising and scanning technologies and the use of numerical data to define medical risk and to make diagnoses. The major difference is that previous technologies that allowed access into the hidden recesses of the body and produced visual or numerical data that reinterpreted and imaged the body's flesh were accessible only to medical practitioners. Patients relied on doctors' authority and command over the data-generating technologies and the risk assessments that informed them how healthy they were (Andersen and Whyte, 2014). Today self-tracking devices allow any users to reinterpret their bodies and render them into data assemblages.

It can therefore be discerned that the representation of data in quantified self-tracking discourses (as least as it was expressed by its progenitors) included several factors from the beginning. These are the notions that the emergence of new digital and mobile devices for gathering information about oneself has facilitated self-tracking and the generation of quantified personal data; that data (and particularly quantified or quantifiable data) are an avenue to self-knowledge; that quantified data are powerful entities; that it is important not only to collect quantified data on oneself, but to analyse these data for the patterns and insights they reveal; that quantifiable data are more neutral, reliable, intellectual and objective than qualitative data, which are intuitive, emotional and subjective; that self-tracked data can provide greater insights than the information that people receive from their senses, revealing previously hidden patterns or correlations; that self-tracked data can be motivational phenomena, inspiring action by entering into a feedback loop; that everything can be rendered as data; and that data about individuals are emblematic of their true selves.

Metricisation and the lure of numbers

Quantification is central to the quantified-self discourse and to many other portrayals of self-tracking. In his *New York Times* article, Gary Wolf expounds on the virtues of numbers: 'We tolerate the pathologies of quantification – a dry, abstract, mechanical type of knowledge – because the results are so powerful. Numbering things allows tests, comparisons, experiments. Numbers make problems less resonant emotionally but more tractable intellectually' (Wolf, 2010).

Generating numbers about oneself has an integral role to play in the data practices and materialisations of many self-trackers. An example of this can be found in the words of John Halamka, an American emergency-care physician and the CIO (chief information officer) of a medical centre who is promoting the use of personal health data from self-tracking as part of healthcare. In an online news item he was quoted as observing:

> You can look at my iPhone and say, 'Oh, over the last week I walked 80,000 steps, my weight's 170, my percentage of body fat is 8 percent. I'm sleeping 4 hours a night which is deep sleep followed by punctuated light sleep, followed by getting up once ... I now have from a $100 device a complete understanding of activity of daily living and my basic functions as a human. (John Halamka, quoted in Comstock, 2014)

In contemporary western societies, numbers have a certain power and resonance. As recent sociological analyses around questions of measure and value have argued, there has been a huge increase generally in the use of metrics in many aspects of social life, which has been greatly impelled by the development of digital technologies for gathering data and for achieving quantification. Scholars have pointed out that there is a politics of measurement: numbers are not neutral, despite the accepted concept of them as devoid of value judgements, assumptions and meanings. The ways in which phenomena are quantified and interpreted and the purposes to which these measurements are put are always implicated in social relationships, power dynamics and ways of seeing. Like any other forms of knowledge, they are social constructions: political, messy and not only reflective but also constitutive of subjects, identities and communities (Adkins and Lury, 2011; Cheney-Lippold, 2011; Day, Lury, and Wakeford, 2014; Gerlitz and Lury, 2014; Ruppert, 2011).

The rationales of both commerce and government are supported by discourses of datification. Concepts of citizenship and consumers are now frequently phrased via the discourses of metricisation and big data, as governments and private enterprises laud the apparent benefits they offer. Publics are rendered manageable, calculable and governable by the metrics that are configured through the algorithmic analysis of personal data. It is assumed that, as long as efficient systems are put in place that are able to gather, share and interpret these data, this process will lead to greater governmental efficiency and to the flourishing of business enterprises as a result of the production of better knowledges about citizens as consumers.

Some scholars use the term 'commensuration' to describe the process by which different qualities are transformed into a common metric, which thus creates relations between these qualities that may not have been previously established or noticed and that may previously have been viewed as fundamentally different from one another. Commensuration confers homogeneity over heterogeneity, and therefore is fundamentally relative (Espeland and Stevens, 1998). Commensuration is a social process, producing new forms of knowledges and understandings. It is political, symbolic and generative, working to reduce complexities and to make differences easier to understand and compare by condensing information. It is a way of managing uncertainty and risk, of securing legitimacy and of imposing control over disorder or chaos (Espeland and Stevens, 1998; Sellar, 2014).

Commensuration has a role to play in many of the scores that are generated by social media platforms and self-tracking devices. In addition to the data that are routinely offered to users of social media platforms about responses to their content, many third-party digital tools have been developed that allow people to view and evaluate in further detail their social media influence and engagement statistics (Gerlitz and Lury, 2014). They use commensuration to develop scores for the purpose of users' self-evaluation. One example in relation to self-tracking cultures is combining various bodily and geographical attributes in a fitness app – heart rate and kilometres covered, for example – in order to produce a single score that is deemed to represent physical exertion. Nike Fuelband users, for instance, receive NikeFuel points that are algorithmically generated and incorporate a range of physical activities into the points calculation: 'from your morning workout to your big night out', as the Nike Fuelband description on the Apple Store puts it (Apple Store Nike Fuelband, 2015).

An example of commensuration as it operates in relation to online engagement is the Klout Score, a measure of influence on social media and other online forums that is recalculated each day. Individuals are given a score out of 100 that is generated from multiple pieces of data from social media platforms, search engines and platforms such as Wikipedia. These pieces are combined by using an algorithm to produce the Klout Score from 1 to 100 (the last time I checked the Klout website, the highest scorers were Barak Obama, with a Klout Score of 99, and Justin Bieber, with one of 92). Many different types of online interactions involving different types of responses (for example tweets, retweets, followers, mentions, list memberships on Twitter, Facebook update statuses, wall posts, friends' 'likes') are homogenised for the purpose of generating the Klout Score.

Gerlitz and Lury (2014: 175) note that such forms of social media scoring not only provide current evaluations of users' influence and popularity but also generate predictive calculations about how these evaluations may change over time, creating, in the authors' words, 'climates of futurity'. This is an important point in relation to self-tracking. Self-tracking technologies involve past or real-time information about the users' activities, but many digital platforms and apps can now make predictions and users are encouraged to strive towards achieving future goals and targets. Users may be invited to peruse the information provided by platforms such as Crowdbooster or Tweetstats (both of which generate statistics about the users' influence on Twitter) to improve their engagement scores (Gerlitz and Lury, 2014). Such metrics, however, tend to leave out certain qualities or attributes in favour of others and to simplify complex human behaviours and responses. Forms of commensuration may begin to take precedence over ways of assessing value and worth, because of their association with rationality and their support of the notion that all value is relative and can be standardised; hence the notion of intrinsic value and other absolute forms of value are denied (Espeland and Stevens, 1998).

The algorithmic manipulation of people's bodily functions and behavioural activities into metrics and scores has significant implications for configuring new types of knowledge about humans. The body/self, as it is produced through self-tracking, is therefore both subject and product of scientific measurement and interpretation. As people's bodily states and functions become ever more recordable and visualised via data displays, it becomes easier to trust the 'numbers'. As I observed in an analysis of sexual activity and reproductive self-tracking apps (Lupton, 2015c), using these technologies encourages people to think about their bodies and their selves through numbers. Sexual activity becomes reduced to 'the numbers': how long intercourse lasts for, how often it takes place, how many thrusts are involved, the volume of sound emitted by participants, how good it is, with how many partners and so on. The comparisons with other users that some of these apps allow for emphasise the notion of sexual experience as a performance, as an activity that can and should be compared with the sexual experiences of others, since they are all rendered into digital data form. These technologies therefore act to support and reinforce highly reductive and normative ideas of what is 'good sex' and 'good performance' by encouraging users to quantify their sexual experiences and feelings in ever finer detail and to represent these data visually, in graphs and tables. The discourses of performance, quantification and normality suggest specific, limited types of sexuality.

So, too, in apps that are designed for women to track their menstrual and ovulation cycles, the rhetoric used both to promote the apps and in their own text suggests that they allow women, by observing and recording their bodies' signs, symptoms and sensations with the help of 'data science', to achieve a greater level of knowledge about their bodies than they otherwise might. These technologies configure a certain type of approach to understanding and experiencing one's body, an algorithmic subjectivity, in which the body and its states of health, functions and activities are portrayed and presented predominantly via quantified calculations, predictions and comparisons. They also work to externalise sexuality and reproductive capacities by turning them into digital data and making them visible and sharable. Thus quantified and digitised in these apps, the messy and multiple complexities, sensual experiences, perversities and quirky contradictions of sexual and reproductive desires and capacities are rendered flat, one-dimensional and dull, subjected as they are to rigid normalised categories.

Data spectacles: Materialisations
of personal data

As I discussed in the previous chapter, creativity and playfulness can be important features of self-tracking practices, particularly those involving gamification. But these features may
also be involved in creating personal data visualisations and
other forms of sharing insights, such as giving talks, as part
of self-tracking. An integral aspect of self-tracking for many
participants is the opportunity it gives them to represent their
personal data in various ways and to 'make sense' of these
data via such representations. In the show and tell of the
Quantified Self movement, whose ethos underpins the movement's 'sharing' mentality, finding compelling visual modes
to demonstrate the patterns in a person's data is a central
feature. The Quantified Self website is full of members' demonstrations of their data, including videos of their show-and-
tell presentations and still images of their visualisations: over
750 such presentations have been uploaded to the site thus
far. Numbers, graphs and charts are common ways of representing personal data, but more qualitative visualisations are
also employed, for instance through the use of word clouds,
colours that stand for moods, and images from photographs
and videos.

Visual representations of data can be highly attractive,
whether they are digitally generated or produced through
time-honoured methods such as drawing, painting, sculpting
and other forms of artistic expression. The American designer
Nicholas Felton is well known for the glossy books he publishes each year, which detail his self-tracked data in attractive
graphical representations (see Feltron.com, 2015). The notion
that data can be beautiful and aesthetically pleasing when
presented in appropriate formats pervades data science in
general: Melissa Gregg (2015) refers to this phenomenon as
the 'data spectacle'. The aesthetic elements of data visualisations involve affective responses that may contain both pleasure and anxiety. Indeed McCosker and Wilken (2014)
identify the tendency, in data visualisation circles, towards
sublimity and the fetishising of 'beautiful data' as part of
exerting mastery over the seemingly unlimited and thus over-

whelming amounts of big digital data sets. Extending this logic, the physical materialisation of digital data in the form of a 2D or 3D data materialisation may offer a solution to the anxieties raised by big data. When it is one's personal data, drawn from one's own flesh, that are being manifested in a material digital data object, this phenomenon may provoke a sense of mastery over what is probably experienced as a continually data-emitting subjectivity. The liquidity, flows and force of personal digital data become frozen in time and space, offering an opportunity to make sense of one's data.

Potent emotional responses can be generated by self-trackers to their own data visualisations and materialisations. In their analysis of interview data from Finnish people who use self-monitoring devices for physical activity and heart-rate tracking, Ruckenstein and Pantzar observe that, when participants were shown the graphs produced from their heart rates, new kinds of affective ties were generated between users and their personal data (Pantzar and Ruckenstein, 2015; Ruckenstein, 2014). The two authors suggest that visual representations of personal data are vital if participants are to respond to the data with high levels of engagement and interest. When a specific part of the body is being closely monitored and its data are visualised and displayed to the owner, this bodily part may become invested with new significance. Similarly, numbers can acquire new significance and emotional meaning because they are measuring elements of one's own body.

For many participants in this study, being able to see from the graphs how many steps they had taken, or how their heart rate had responded to exercise, or how well they had slept was motivating and pleasurable. The well-rested body, as demonstrated by an undisturbed night's rest evidenced by heart-rate data, was viewed as an achievement, an accomplishment of the body – as was the tired body that resulted from a highly active day. Activities such as housework gained new value because they contributed positively to exercise and heart-rate data, while stress-alleviating activities, as demonstrated via graphs, were also valued for their contribution to rest and recovery (which resulted in a lowered heart rate). These embodied feelings gained additional value from the data visualisations that 'proved' and supported them, thus engendering pleasurable emotions such as satisfaction and a sense of accomplishment.

Ruckenstein and Pantzar found that the participants in their study viewed the data visualisations as more credible and accurate than the 'subjective' assessments of their bodily sensations; indeed they expressed the desire for more data about their bodies to add to those already collected, so as to gain further insights. Several participants commented that the visualisations revealed aspects of their lives that they may have suspected (such as the stressful nature of their work), but the data served to prove these impressions, while others found that the data demonstrated findings that they had not anticipated (they were more physically active than they thought). A new kind of value was therefore given to some everyday activities and interactions.

Artistic and design interventions

Artists and designers have experimented with various ways of materialising personal data beyond the standard graph or list of numbers. An exhibition of artistic responses to lifelogging held at Chicago's Elmhurst Art Museum in 2014 (Elmhurst Art Museum, 2014) included people who used photographic or painted self-portraits, the market and sentimental value of objects they owned or things they carried while travelling and translated longitude and latitude data of their daily spatial location into kinetic sculptures or weather data into woven sculptures and musical scores. Data artist Laurie Frick has developed her FRICKbits Data Art app, the purpose of which is to encourage self-trackers to '[t]ake back your data and turn it into art' and to 'make the ultimate data-selfie' (Frick, 2015). She has used various materials for portraying the personal information she has collected on herself, including her 'Floating Data' project. This project involved Frick's use of laser cut anodised aluminium panels to display the details of her walking data, which she describes as a 'human data portrait' (Floating Data, 2015). Audiences can view, touch and walk past these panels.

One example of using analogue drawing techniques to represent personal data is the 'Dear Data' data drawing project conducted by Giorgia Lupi and Stefanie Posavec (Dear Data, 2015). For a one-year period these women, living in cities on different continents (Europe and North America), engaged in tracking information about themselves each week and then drawing and writing about their data on a large postcard, which they would send to each other. Their weekly self-tracking topics were quirky, including such features as 'a week of clocks', 'a week of mirrors' and 'a week of complaints'. On the blog they put together to describe and represent the project, they observe that this data collection and visualisation practice 'became a sort of performance and ritual in our lives, affecting our days and weeks, and inherently changing our behaviour' (Dear Data, 2015).

A range of creative expressions of and challenges to personal data has been exhibited or displayed on artists' websites. For some artists, their collection, interpretation and display of personal data are a response to the imperative that impels other self-trackers. However, their impulse, in contrast to that of many self-trackers, is not necessarily to collect and display 'truthful' data, but rather to reflect on the practice and its implications for concepts of the self and the body. In 2002 British designer and researcher Lucy Kimbell created a performance art piece entitled 'LIX Index' that involved her uploading 50 pieces of her personal data into a database (LIX Index, 2002; see also LIX Index, 2014). These pieces included such elements as her bank balance, hours spent outdoors, the air temperature where she lives, conversations with friends and family, tweets, orgasms, physical activity and intellectual stimulation. She produced a weekly index from these disparate sources of data, the LIX Index (an example of commensuration that I discussed in Chapter 4). Kimbell's blog discusses the difficulties and surprises involved in making and engaging with her index. Her first iteration of the LIX Index lasted a year. She then started again in 2012 for some months, but apparently grew tired very quickly of doing it. On her blog, which recounts her more recent experiences of creating the LIX Index, Kimbell discusses the tedium of collecting and uploading her personal information and her attitude that such an enterprise represents a 'neurotic data gathering' (LIX

Index, 2015). Her work questions the purpose of collecting such personal information and the criteria that are used to evaluate its worth and that of the self-tracker, as well as exposing the messiness involved in self-tracking.

In addition to artistic interventions, practitioners in the field of critical making have developed some responses to the collection and use of personal information in the digital data economy. 'Critical making' is a phrase that is used to denote the unification of creative and engineering practices with critical social theory. The making of material objects and representational (art) works can provide a means of engaging with social issues by bringing together theoretical concepts and the design and engineering of material artefacts. This is seen as a form of intervention into dominant knowledge systems. It includes approaches such as participatory design, critical technical practice, critical or reflexive design and tactical media. Some writers also use the descriptions 'design fiction' or 'speculative design' to denote ways of imagining alternatives to technologies and technological practices (Dunne and Raby, 2013; Galloway, 2013).

As Oron Catts and Ionat Zurr, both practitioners of design fiction, put it, some creative efforts 'offer glimpses of the possible and the contestable; works that are neither utopic or [sic] dystopic but rather ambiguous and messy' (quoted in Turney, 2015). The idea is not to present concepts that are feasible or practical, but to 'invite new kinds of conversations about technological futures' (Turney, 2015). Inviting these new kinds of conversations might seek to reincorporate (in both senses of the word) the sensory knowledge of the self. As I have contended in this book, the knowledges that are generated about bodies and selves by conventional digitised self-tracking devices may appear to be clean and uncontaminated in their sheer digitisation. Yet numbers and graphs as a source of knowledge serve to represent bodies and selves in very limited, impoverished ways. Compare these flat forms of data materialisations with the complexities of the affective embodied knowledge that constitutes a response to a scent, a taste, a sound or the touch of skin.

Some design and artistic work is attempting to bring these elements of corporeal sensation into data practices and materialisations related to self-tracking. Examples of this type of work were included in the 2014 'Grow Your Own: Life after Nature' exhibition at Trinity College Dublin (Trinity College Dublin Science Gallery, 2015). This exhibition was directed at displayed design work and aimed to invite people to consider the implications of synthetic biology – a scientific experimental process that concerns genetic engineering. The projects presented 'living machines' that resulted from collaborations between engineers, scientists, designers, artists and biohackers. It asked such questions as 'how might designed life merge into our own? Where is the boundary between our things and our selves; the designed products that we consume, and our own bodies and identities?' (Trinity College Dublin Science Gallery, 2015). Such questions, as I have argued in this book, are also central to understanding self-tracking cultures and practices.

One of the projects on display is the 'self-made' human cheese project by Christina Agapakis and Sissel Tolaas. This project involved using human microbiota (in other words, bacteria that live in the human body) taken from the skin of several people to culture cheeses, each of which had developed from the specific microflora of these people. The exhibition displayed these cheeses to the public and invited its members to smell the individual microbial projects. Just as each human body has a unique microbial collection, so too the cheese that is made from each person's microbes emits a unique odour. This project therefore highlights the intersections between individual features of people's bodies – features of which they may not be overtly aware – and how these data – in this case, their unique skin microbial collection – may be converted into another material form and identified by others via the sense of smell (Agapakis and Tolaas, 2014).

In another exhibition, by Heather Dewey-Hagborg and entitled 'Stranger Visions', the artist created portrait sculptures from the analysis of human genetic material that she collected from public places: specifically, DNA (desoxyribonucleic acid) that had been left on cigarette butts discarded in the streets of Dublin. She used elements of the genomic profile that was created from this DNA – namely elements related to physical traits – to print out a 3D model of the person's face, in an attempt to imagine his or her appearance. Dewey-Hagborg's intention was to provoke audiences into contemplating the possibility that people's DNA could be taken from detritus that they had unknowingly left behind and their identity inspected (Dewey-Hagborg, 2012–13). In her work, Dewey-Hagborg displays a collection of her own bodily products, which she has gathered over a 24-hour period (A Day in the Life, 2014). These include hair left in her brush, used tissues and nail clippings. These ephemera are used to stimulate reflection on the ways in which such objects can be analysed for DNA (by oneself or others), as a form of self-tracking or as a mode of surveillance exerted by others. As Dewey-Hagborg's work suggests, as material objects become invested over time with the marks of our use, they too can become data: repositories of information and sources of inspiration for reflection about ourselves and our lives.

Designers are beginning to use 3D printing technologies as a way of rendering people's digital data into three-dimensional forms that can be touched. Rohit Khot and colleagues (Khot, Hjorth, and Mueller, 2014), for example, have investigated the use of 3D printing to produce material artefacts that represent an individual's heart rate during physical exertion. The idea of such artefacts is to encourage people to achieve greater awareness of their personal data and to engage in self-reflection upon being confronted with the material representation of these data. Previously this kind of stimulus through objects has been confined to artwork installations, scientific experiments and education rather than extending over people's interpretations of the meanings of data (Stusak, Tabard, Sauka, Khot, and Butz, 2014). Khot, Hjorth and Mueller (2014) argue that, as any given physical activity is a material, embodied practice, material representations of the data related to this activity – representations that can be handled and touched – help people to make sense of their data. They characterise this approach as employing a 'physical–digital–physical' mode of interaction, 'where physical energy is first invested in generating data such as heart rate, which is then converted back to a material form, re-entering the physical world' (Khot, Hjorth et al., 2014: 2).

Khot, Hjorth and Mueller tested their system, entitled SweatAtoms, via six households that used five different material manifestations of their physical activity. These artefacts included a 3D graph of heart-rate data, a flower shape where the length and width of the petals represented heart-rate duration and intensity, a frog shape that changed in size according to the amount of physical activity carried out during one day, a die representing the six zones of heart-beat data, and a ring displaying the number of active hours in a day. The participants were supplied with a digital heart-rate monitor, an iPod Touch endowed with an app for collecting the data, and a 3D printer for their homes to print out the artefacts from their data. The researchers found that viewing and handling the objects helped people gain a sense of their bodily data and illustrated different levels of engagement with these data. They concluded from their investigations: 'we envision people crafting their world with moments from their lives, using data that was [sic] previously only seen in digital form but now re-entering their physical world in an embodied material form' (Khot, Hjorth et al., 2014: 9). They found that the emotional connections that people had with their personal data were strengthened by the ability to handle these objects.

With other collaborators (Stusak et al., 2014) Khot has explored the idea of 'activity sculptures' – 3D printed sculptures made from physical activity data (running) extracted from popular apps. The data included the duration of a run, the distance covered, the average speed and the calories burned. The sculptures include a figure, a necklace, a lamp and a jar. Each individual piece represents a specific run by a participant in the study. The approach these designers adopt contends that encouraging people to engage with their data should be playful and emotionally appealing. These researchers recruited 14 participants with varying levels of running experience (some had none at all) and engaged them in the sculptures that were made from their running data over a three-week period. The sculptures were produced off-site and then given to the participants as if they were rewards. They were designed to be modular, so that separate pieces were given after each run to be formed together; the purpose was to make the sculpture into a further incentive for participants to continue to engage in their runs.

Here again, participants exhibited some interesting responses to the sculptures that were based on their activity data. Several found the pieces decorative and evocative, and also as clearly representing variations in their running activities. Some enjoyed fitting the various pieces together, comparing them with other participants' pieces or displaying or wearing them. The researchers noted that such factors as curiosity, playfulness and aesthetics began to influence the ways in which the participants planned their runs, as they tried to control the shape of the pieces they would receive from each run or experimented with how certain aspects of their runs might influence the shape or size of the pieces that eventuated.

Khot is now working on using food 3D printing technologies to render bodily data into edible objects that can be consumed. He and colleagues (Khot, Lee, Munz, Aggarwal, and Mueller, 2014) have experimented with a system they call 'TastyBeats', which creates a unique, personalised drink by using heart-beat data from an individual engaged in physical activity. The height of the jet of the drink fountain used and the flavours that are produced for the drink are influenced by the heart rate of the individuals who contribute their data. The proposed system may be used to construct personalised energy drinks that can customise the contents on the basis of the physical activity data of each user. In this concept such aspects as the colour and flavour of the fluid produced by the drink fountain as well as the intensity of the liquid flow in the fountain act to represent the physical data in sensory ways. Khot and collaborators Ryan Pennings and Floyd Mueller from the RMIT Exertion Games Lab are also working on a project named 'Edi-Pulse' (originally 'Sweet-Hearts'), which transforms self-tracked heart-rate data into 3D chocolate materialisations. The idea is to reward people for engaging in physical activity with a chocolate that represents the level of exertion to which they have engaged in it. The energy expended in exercise is converted into food energy, which then acts to create more energy in the body (Millsaps, 2014).

Another design researcher, Stephen Barrass, has used a different technique, acoustic sonification, to render personal self-tracked data into objects, or 'as a medium for telling stories about numbers' (Barrass, 2014: 1). He used his own data from a year of blood-pressure monitoring to produce a version of a Tibetan singing bowl – what he calls the Hypertension Singing Bowl. The bowl was fabricated from stainless steel by using 3D printing. The act of rubbing the inside of the bowl with a special stick produces a musical sound. Barrass' personal bodily data are therefore configured into an object that both is visual and tactile and can produce a unique sound. Each set of data produces a bowl that is slightly different in its proportions, and therefore in its acoustic properties. Barrass argues that not only can people see and hear this physical manifestation of their blood-pressure readings, they can also use the sound as a reflective stimulus that helps them calm their bodies and therefore reduce high blood pressure. This data object can therefore act as both a representation of personal data and an intervention in the type of data that are subsequently generated.

The importance of context

I have remarked above on the value that is given to metricisation in accounts of the quantified self and other self-tracking practices. However, in recent years there has been evidence of a growing cynicism in some popular outlets concerning the value of the data gained from metrics. As expressed in an article for *The Huffington Post*, it can be difficult to discern the meaning and value of one's data. The author further notes that simply 'knowing your number' may not be enough to change a person's behaviour:

> We can visualize the data we collect from countless gadgets, but will we understand what the data means [*sic*]? Even if you know your retirement 'number' does that knowledge empower you or unnerve you? How does the data [*sic*] vary under a variety of conditions and factors? For example, does a rapid heart rate indicate an underlying disease or did you forget that before you downloaded the data you ran up the stairs to access the web as fast as you could to use that new supercool health visualization app? (Coughlin, 2014)

From this perspective, numbers alone tell us nothing. It is the contexts in which numbers (or any other forms of data

about the self) are created that are important. As two designers put it:

> context humanizes the numbers and places them back into
> our lives in meaningful ways. For example, a fitness tracker
> can tell us that our physical activity is down from the previous
> month. But it cannot tell us that the inactivity is due to a
> sprained ankle. Given that context, those declining numbers
> might tell a different story: that we are recovering steadily
> rather than slacking off. Even in that simple scenario, it is
> clear that a small bit of context can frame data in a much
> more insightful way. (Boam and Webb, 2014)

An example of the importance of context in relation to personal data is given by a man who identifies himself on his
blog only as 'Morris' (Morris, 2014). Morris uses a Narrative
mini-camera clipped to his clothes to take photos automatically throughout the day. In a blog post he reflects on what
he does with the digitised images that are stored in his Narrative folder. After six months of use, Morris has over 200,000
images in his folder. He bought the camera to get assistance
in his daily journaling, where he writes down everything that
has happened to him that day. The images taken by the
camera serve as an aide-memoire, reminding him of 'what I
have done and what I have left to do'. The photos also serve
to make him more aware 'of how many people I see every
day but do not interact with'. Morris remarks that reviewing
his images

> has given me another feeling of community that I did not quite
> realize. There are so many other people out there, in the street,
> in the metro, that pass through the same environments and
> that are mostly like me in the end. I recognize some of them
> now in the street, in the metro, and I feel more of a sensation
> of community, closeness. (Morris, 2014)

Morris observes that, if he had not photographed these people
regularly and reviewed the photos at the end of each day, he
would not have recognised them again. This would have led
to his feeling more anonymous as he walked through those
public spaces, 'possibly more an independent object in a
colder world' (Morris, 2014).

These types of observations go well beyond reacting to 'counting' or 'numbers'. They are affective responses to everyday interactions, responses based on the interpretation of the content of images. Indeed, as I remarked in Chapter 3, people respond emotionally to the data they generate from self-tracking, and their emotions may be highly evident in how they display or talk about their data. The intimacy of revealing one's personal details to others is part of the context in which they are gathered and displayed. The format of the 'show and tell' on the Quantified Self website is directed at asking people to explain the following aspects of their self-tracking practices: 'What did you do? How did you do it? What did you learn?' (2014 QS Europe Conference, 2014). These talks open a window on often very private aspects of people's lives: how they are dealing with grief at the loss of a family member, coping with a chronic illness or attempting to give up smoking or lose weight, how long they sit in front of their computer, at what times they go to bed and wake up, how parenthood had changed their lives, what their dreams and their moods are. Therefore, for those who choose to share their data, whether during a show and tell at a meeting or online, there is a strong confessional dimension: 'These are my data; this is what these data reveal about me.'

Sharing one's data has implications not only for how users view and understand their own bodies but for how other members of the quantified-self community view and respond to them. The practice of quantifying the self, in this context, is not merely about monitoring and measuring oneself. It is also, and centrally, about communicating dimensions of the self by using visual or other material based on one's data, about seeking to help others see and understand patterns in the data and perhaps make connections to their own data in productive ways. Selecting when and to whom to reveal these details of their personal lives and the extent to which they themselves wish to be reminded of them can be significant choices for self-trackers.

An important aspect of the troves of personal data that are collected about people as part of self-tracking is the extent to which they constantly remind them of events and times of their lives. For some, these may be painful memories, which they would rather forget (Allen, 2008; Sellen and Whittaker, 2010). This dimension of self-tracking is articulated in a blog post by Rachel Metz, who writes:

> there were some moments captured by my life-logging cameras that I'd rather not relive, like one particularly stressful Saturday night I spent at the wood shop helping my fiancé, Noah, finish up a project. The Narrative Clip's camera captured hours of exhaustion and irritation as we fumbled to glue little pieces of wood into small slots cut out of a giant map. I had pretty much forgotten about that miserable night until I glanced back at a set of images that show Noah in the corner of the frame with a sad look on his face. Every time I look at it, I wince. (Metz, 2014)

Self-trackers may not be able to control the extent to which they come face to face with personal details that they would rather forget. The concept of 'inadvertent algorithmic cruelty' was introduced in a blog post by Eric Meyer (2014), who wrote movingly about how Facebook's 'Your Year in Review' – a function that is offered to users – distressed him. That year his young daughter Rebecca had died. Meyer avoided participating in that function (which is optional), but was still given continual reminders by Facebook, and some messages used images of his dead daughter. He was unable to avoid these constant reminders of his loss.

Some commentators seek to describe the concept of the 'qualified self' as a practice involving reflection and the interpretation of information, whether the latter is in the form of numbers or not. The qualified self involves the interpretation and assessment of any form of data – a reflexive engagement with this information that seeks to contextualise it in relation to other forms of data. The practice of self-tracking can therefore be regarded as a way of thinking information through as well as thinking *with* it, working to make connections between one kind or source and others. The validity or the quality of the information is interrogated: 'Where the *quantified* self gives us raw numbers, the *qualified* self completes our understanding of those numbers. The second half completes the first half' (Boam and Webb, 2014). Davis (2013) has similarly contended:

This qualitative component is key in mediating between raw numbers and identity meanings. If self-quantifiers are seeking self-knowledge through numbers, then narratives and subjective interpretations are the mechanisms by which data morphs into selves. Self-quantifiers don't just use data to learn about themselves, but rather, use data to construct the stories that they tell themselves about themselves.

When self-tracking is viewed in this way, what is important for self-trackers is the range of the information that can be gathered about themselves, the specific types of information they choose to collect, and the process of making sense of this information. Davis refers to the 'stories that [self-trackers] tell about themselves'; but self-tracking is also about the stories that people tell others, or the types of selves that are presented to others. Indeed, as I asserted in Chapter 3, the very act of self-tracking, or positioning oneself as a self-tracker, is already a performance of a certain type of subject: the reflexive self-monitoring subject.

This distinction between the quantified and the qualified self works towards challenging the notion of 'the quantified self'. Indeed it may be contended that the essential feature of the quantified self, at least as it is described in the motto 'self knowledge by numbers', is self-knowledge, however it is produced. Here the word 'numbers' really comes to stand for 'information of any kind about oneself', and 'self-knowledge' means not only the accumulation of facts about oneself and the interpretation of these facts, but also a heightened recognition of the implications of confronting one's personal information and sharing it with others. Collecting and aggregating personal data therefore contribute to a range of practices that involve self-knowledge, self-expression and sometimes the unburdening of weighty emotions or private insights about the self. Self-tracking becomes performative, both for the insights that a self-tracker may achieve about her or his life and in terms of the aesthetics of the data that she or he may be able to curate and the decisions the self-tracker makes about which information to voluntarily share with others, which to keep private and which to try to ignore or avoid.

The discussion in this chapter has focused on personal data meanings and practices. The data produced by self-trackers are generally represented as 'small' and human-made, wrought from the personalised decisions and individual objectives of the people who gather them. Yet, if these data are generated by digital devices, they are often aggregated into big data sets and become part of the digital data economy. This raises issues about data politics, security and privacy in terms of the ways in which people's personal details are accessed by other parties. These issues are the focus of the next chapter.

5

'Data's Capacity for Betrayal'
Personal Data Politics

In the previous chapter I discussed the ways in which self-trackers seek to make sense of, materialise and use their personal information. Beyond these reflexive data practices, some self-trackers confront the next level of data use: where and how their personal data are stored, how they are harvested by other actors, what these actors do with their data and how they can gain better access to them. This chapter addresses these political dimensions of personal data.

Exploited self-tracking

Several years ago, when digital technologies were beginning to be used for self-tracking, Dodge and Kitchin (Dodge and Kitchin, 2007; Kitchin and Dodge, 2011) raised some important questions about the data that are produced through lifelogging practices. Here are some of their questions: Who (other than the creator) should have access to the data archives that are preserved in a lifelog? Should other people, whose data may be included in an individual's data archives, have access to some or all of the data contained in those archives (for example, images of them or details about them?) To what extent could the material be sequestered for legal cases? To what extent would deletion of data or suspension of data gathering from a lifelog be considered a sign of guilt if the lifelog were to be used in a legal case? Could other actors insert false information into a person's lifelog, thus creating false memories? What happens to lifelog data after the death of the creator? What are the inheritance rights? How much more valid than human memories are these data to be considered? How long will lifelogs remain an act of choice and free will – will their collection become mandatory and be imposed by (some) authorities? Should portions of a lifelog be available for erasing or modifying? What details should be preserved? Is there a need to forget misfortunes and errors? What happens if one's lifelog data are stolen and used by others? Who has control over a child's lifelog?

An important implication of automated digital recording of a greater amount of personal information is that such technologies lack the power to discriminate. They simply continue to record details, leaving no sign or mark of what is important, which details should be preserved and which could be relinquished (Kitchin and Dodge, 2011). Dodge and Kitchin (2007: 439) contend that lifelogs have the potential to fulfil a 'marketer's dream' – if that marketer is able to get access to the wealth of personal details in a lifelog, including the self-tracker's purchasing and consumption habits. The two authors envisage incidents in which third parties might use this information for social sorting, invasive profiling and disciplining. They raise the possibility of insurance companies and other commercial entities requiring access to lifelog data for the benefit of calculating risks and premiums or for the purpose of according preferential treatment to some customers – while others, who fit certain profiles, would be penalised. Dodge and Kitchin also identify the possibility that society would become more conservative once people are aware that their personal information can be accessed by others and used against them, thus making public forbidden, indiscreet or criminal behaviours.

Dodge and Kitchin were writing before the widespread use of cloud computing, the growth in the collection and use of personal data by internet companies such as Facebook, Amazon and Google and the spreading of self-tracking practices beyond the realm of the private and the consensual. The uses of the personal data that people have generated through self-tracking – that is, the uses that Dodge and Kitchin envisaged several years ago – have largely eventuated as the two authors predicted.

I have referred throughout this book to the notion of 'lively data', as the feature involved in this notion participates in the digital data economy. As I have argued, one dimension of the vitality of digital data relates to the multiple ways in which different actors and agencies may use them for their own purposes. This multiplicity has major implications for how the information that people collect about themselves, as part of self-tracking endeavours, is used (or indeed misused) by others. The exploitation of people's personal information by second and third parties is a significant political issue, not simply because of the data privacy and security issues involved but also because of the ways in which people's personal information has become valuable for these parties. The collection of personal data is now not only a mode of consensual, individually driven imperatives for self-improvement, but also an element of (sometimes illegal) commercial profiteering, population monitoring and governance.

Indeed one might view the knowledges that are created through self-tracking practices as a new element of biopower or vitality expertise. The movement of self-tracking cultures into commercial, managerial and government domains combines the rationalities of biocapital with those of the digital data economy. Biocapital involves the derivation of value from biological entities such as human bodies (Rose, 2008), while the digital data economy positions digital data objects as valuable. Just as other forms of human life – such as human gametes, blood, tissues and cells – have become commodified and invested with monetary value, so too have the digital data assemblages that are configured on human bodies via self-tracking. Indeed the value attributed to personal digital data assemblages combines two kinds of value: one related to the digital data economy and one emerging from the capitalisation of the human body. Many self-tracking practices involve the rendering of bodily attributes and dispositions into digital data. They produce value in terms of the intimate biodigital knowledges that they generate from individuals, and therefore self-tracking practices may be described as generating digital biocapital.

The creation of digital content – that is, prosumption on online platforms and apps – can be viewed as a form of work. Indeed some scholars have represented prosumption in general as free digital labour, in which people who generate these data do so for the commercial benefit of other actors and agencies. Their labour is exploited because, while they may benefit personally from their acts of prosumption (for example, by enjoying free access to platforms and apps and opportunities to interact with others, use the information provided there, or monitor their bodies and behaviours closely), others are profiting financially from this freely given content (Fuchs and Dyer-Witheford, 2013; Rey, 2012; Till, 2014). People are not offered financial compensation, nor do they receive it for providing their experiences. The value that prosumers derive is noncommercial, while the exchange value of the data they create is accumulated by the for-profit companies that provide the platforms for people to share their experiences or to trawl the web, harvest the data and render it into a form that is valuable for commercial entities.

The exploitation of prosumers' personal information frequently occurs when people use apps and other software for self-tracking. Many commercial companies are interested in the type of details about health, physical activities and consumption patterns that are revealed by the information collected by self-trackers on their bodies and lives (Till, 2014). For example, when people engage in user experience platforms such as PatientsLikeMe, they are encouraged to share the information they have collected about their bodies, medical conditions and treatments with other patients with the same condition. These data are valuable not only to other patients, for the insights they offer them, but also to the platform developers, who on-sell these data, and to other third parties, who use them for research into medical conditions, for clinical trials of new pharmaceuticals, or for purely commercial purposes – as do medical device manufacturers and pharmaceutical companies, for instance (Lupton, 2014).

The burgeoning business of data harvesting and data brokering involves a process whereby companies are scraping the web for whatever they can find about people; in other words it involves the sale of the data that have been generated through the use of apps and other software. Data-harvesting and brokering companies use the information they can find online or have bought from developers in order to construct 'profiles' that provide detailed descriptions of the behaviours and health states of the people profiled. Drawing on this information, some companies create lists of people who have been sexually assaulted, diagnosed with a mental health condition or a sexually transmitted disease, designated as impulse buyers or credit risks, or accused of wrongdoing. These lists are sold to marketers, financial institutions and potential employers (Pasquale, 2014).

The advent of big data, together with the opportunity to mine them for personal information, has created new possibilities for social and economic discrimination against the disadvantaged and against minority social groups. Here one could mention the potential for predictive privacy harms, which covers cases where individuals are adversely affected by assumptions and predictions made about them on the basis of preexisting digital data sets (Crawford and Schultz, 2014; Robinson, Yu, and Rieke, 2014). Predictive algorithms that draw on personal digital data are used now in many social and economic domains. This new practice can affect people's access to healthcare, credit, insurance, social security, educational institutions and employment options and render them vulnerable to unfair targeting by policing and security agencies (Crawford and Schultz, 2014; Nuffield Council on Bioethics, 2015; Rosenblat, Kneese, and boyd, 2014). What is more, it can be difficult to challenge such assessments or to seek to have certain personal details removed from digital data sets, even if the data on which they are based are proven to be inaccurate.

Some employers have begun to use the algorithms of specially designed automated software for the purpose of selecting employees; they are also engaging in online searches through search engines or professional networking platforms such as LinkedIn in order to seek out information on job applicants (Rosenblat, Kneese et al., 2014). Now that diverse databases holding personal details on various aspects of people's lives can be joined together for analysis, information on features such as a job applicant's health status or sexual orientation may become identifiable (Andrejevic, 2014). One recent study found that Google directs fewer higher-paid job advertisements to female than to male users in search of employment sites, in a clear case of algorithmic discrimination based on gender (Datta, Tschantz, and Datta, 2015).

Insurance and credit companies are scraping big data sets to develop customer profiles, with the result that disadvantaged groups suffer further disadvantage by being targeted for differential offers or excluded altogether because they are not viewed as profitable or as poor credit risks (Libert, 2014; Robinson et al., 2014). Data brokers in the United States use available personal data to calculate certain predictive 'health scores' on patients with the help of digital data; such scores include the Affordable Care Act (ACA) individual health risk score, which is used for assessing the risk factor for an individual who requires healthcare (Sarasohn-Kahn, 2014). Some American hospitals are purchasing from data-broking companies data on their patients' credit card transactions and information about them in public records and and in customer loyalty programs, in an attempt to use predictive algorithms for creating models that identify 'high-risk' patients. These patients will then be contacted by the hospital as part of an intervention program that seeks to prevent ill health and reduce healthcare admissions (Pettypiece and Robertson, 2014).

The legal implications of the use of personal data archives for evidence are just beginning to emerge. In 2014 the first known case where an individual's self-tracking data (collected by her Fitbit physical activity tracker) were used as legal evidence in a personal injury lawsuit received media attention. A Canadian fitness instructor sought to use her physical activity data, collected by her Fitbit, to demonstrate reduction in her activity after an injury. Her lawyers used the data analytics platform Vivametrica to compare this woman's physical activity data with those of the general population. Commentators on this case speculated that similar self-tracked personal data could be used in the future not only to support people's lawsuits, but also as evidence to prosecute them in litigation (Olson, 2014a).

Pushed and imposed self-tracking

The growing adoption, by actors and agencies, of self-tracking practices and rationales beyond the realm of the consensual and the personal raises questions about the extent to which people are now being pushed or even coerced into taking up self-tracking. Advocates who encourage people to take up self-tracking are particularly visible in the domains of patient self-care, health promotion, preventive medicine and health insurance. In the persuasive computing and digital health literature, the personal data that are generated from self-tracking are represented as pedagogical and motivational – a means of encouraging self-reflection or emotional responses such as fear, guilt or shame that will lead to the desired behavioural changes. While many people may choose to engage in these types of enterprises willingly, as part of their personal goals and motivations, there is abundant evidence in these programs that they are strongly associated with the objective of persuading people who are otherwise reluctant to participate in them. Hence the motivation for self-tracking is viewed as requiring impetus from the external agency that is attempting to change people's behaviour.

Such a perspective on encouraging self-tracking draws on traditional paternalistic approaches to health promotion and health education, in which lay people are positioned as ignorant or lacking motivation and self-control (Crawshaw, 2012; Lupton, 1995b; Petersen and Lupton, 1996). The recent interpretation of this paternalism as 'nudging' (Thaler and Sustein, 2009) adopts an explanatory framework that attempts to preserve a veneer of choice and voluntary behaviour change by making paternalism seem to appeal to strategies that subtly encourage such change. Nudges are designed so that they are not readily obvious to their target groups, or they appear to be easy to respond to without great deliberation or motivation; thus they are viewed as consensual rather than imposed. They may be deceptive or manipulative in the way they achieve their ends. This a type of 'soft' or 'libertarian' paternalism that adheres to the neoliberal model of governing populations, in which coercion is largely replaced by psychological models of behaviour that encourage people to take up self-care practices for their own health, happiness and productivity. At its heart is the belief that, left to themselves, people would not readily take up behaviours deemed to be wise, productive and conducive to the ideal of the responsible entrepreneurial citizen; hence they must be 'encouraged' to do so by other actors and agencies.

Some writers in the field of persuasive computing and in that of nudging design are beginning to discuss the possibility of developing wearable technologies or smart objects that not only monitor people's bodies or interactions but actively intervene to discipline them. An example of such an object would be a desk lamp that turns on only when a smart phone has been placed inside it, to discourage overuse of the phone. It has been suggested that future designs may include a smart sofa that can kick people off it if they have been lounging for too long, or a smart watch that informs users that they should walk to work rather than catching the train and then urges them to walk faster if they fail to demonstrate enough enthusiasm (Peters, 2015). The Apple Watch already notices how often wearers stand and move around, and sends them notifications if they are deemed by its algorithms and sensors to have been sedentary for too long.

More obvious forms of pushing self-tracking on people are appearing in the domain of insurance. Drawing on the possibilities of self-tracking technologies, insurance companies are beginning to adopt the usage-based insurance model, which is predicated on the fact that people provide individualised information to insurers for the calculation of risks and subsequent premiums. This approach to insurance moves from actuarial calculations of risk that are based on aggregated historical data to risk assessments that focus on the individual's characteristics, as derived from a long list of variables (NAIC, 2014). As I observed in Chapter 1, some car insurance companies use telematic driving-monitoring technologies to calculate their clients' risk profiles and premiums. Health and life insurance companies are also beginning to encourage their clients to upload their self-tracking health and fitness data. For example, the insurance company AIA (Acts Interpretation Act) Australia offers a Vitality life insurance program in which, as its website puts it, 'your healthy choices are financially rewarded'. Its clients are encouraged to engage in an array of preventive health, monitoring, testing and screening programs to earn points that will then reduce their premiums. These are divided into 'know your health' and 'improve your health' activities. The 'know your health' activities include completing online tools to calculate aspects of overall health status and mental wellbeing, completing a non-smoker's declaration and seeking health, nutrition, fitness and dental assessments from providers. The 'improve your health' activities involve attending gym or fitness sessions, engaging in 'stop smoking' or weight loss programs, ordering fresh food online, and wearing digital activity wearable devices and uploading the data to the company. Each time they perform these activities, clients earn points that are then used to reduce their premiums.

Other agencies, such as retailers that offer customer loyalty programs, are encouraging their clients to allow them access not only to purchasing behaviours displayed in supermarkets and pharmacies but also to self-tracked health and fitness data, which allows them to combine various forms of data so as to make inferences about their customers' health-related habits and preferences. The Balance Rewards for Healthy Choices program is offered by Walgreens, America's largest pharmacy retailing chain. As part of a customer loyalty program, people are offered the opportunity to 'earn points for your healthy choices', to save money on products, and to 'take advantage of great, exclusive offers for members' (Walgreens, 2014). They can do so by first recording details of their physical activity, chronic disease management or progress towards a health-related goal such as losing weight or ceasing smoking and then syncing the data collected via digital fitness trackers or uploading them onto Walgreens' platform or customised app.

The Australian Coles supermarket chain has a customer loyalty program that incorporates collecting not only information on their members' spending habits in the supermarkets and liquor stores owned by the company but also health and fitness data on them from digital self-tracking devices. The company offers life insurance, and is also associated with a major private health-insurance company that offers benefits to insured clients who regularly upload health and fitness data onto their platform. It is not difficult to envisage a scenario in which data concerning food, cigarette and alcohol purchases and health and medical information are brought together, used to make predictions about consumers, and result in a differential targeting and pricing of insurance packages.

Corporate wellness programs in the American workplace represent an instance where the boundaries between voluntary self-tracking and pushed, or even imposed self-tracking can be blurred. As discussed in Chapter 1, in the United States many employers take responsibility for securing a proportion of their employees' health-insurance coverage; they do this as part of a benefit package, in the absence of nationalised public healthcare systems such as those offered in other western countries. For this reason employers have a financial interest in promoting wellness programs among their staff members in addition to attempting to reduce absenteeism and subsequent productivity loss due to illness. The Affordable Care Act allows American employers to provide financial incentives for their staff members' participation in workplace health-promotion initiatives and demonstrations of progress towards attaining personal health goals – namely incentives in the form of payments of up to 30 per cent of these members' health-insurance premiums (Zamosky, 2014). Wearable technology manufacturers such as Fitbit are brokering deals with employers and insurance companies to sell fitness and activity trackers and data analytics software as part of these wellness programs (Olson, 2014b; Zamosky, 2014).

There is a fine line between consensual, pushed and imposed self-tracking. While some elements of self-interest may still operate and a discourse of 'choice' may be employed, people may have little option of opting out. In the case of workplace wellness programs involving the self-tracking of physical activity or body weight, for instance, wearing the devices and allowing employers to view employees' personal data may be presented as optional. However, failure to participate in the program may lead the enforcement of higher health-insurance premiums by an employer, as is happening in some American workplaces (Olson, 2014b). At its most coercive, imposed self-tracking is used in programs involving the monitoring of location and drug use for probation and parole surveillance, drug-addiction programs, and family law and child-custody monitoring.

Personal data security and privacy

There are many significant issues concerning the security and privacy of the personal information that self-trackers upload to apps and other software. Developers often fail to inform users that their data are available to third parties (Ackerman, 2013; Sarasohn-Kahn, 2014). In the United States, where many internationally popular apps are developed, there are no legal requirements that app developers provide privacy policy statements in their information for users. A recent study of privacy policies on mobile health- and fitness-related apps found that many lacked any kind of privacy policy, few took steps to encrypt the data collected, and many sent such data to a third party not disclosed by the developer on its website (Ackerman, 2013).

The US Federal Trade Commission found that 12 free health and fitness apps focusing on relevant behaviours or on conditions such as smoking cessation, physical activity and pregnancy shared user data with a total of 76 third parties. These data in some cases included geolocation, gender, names and email addresses, exercise and diet habits and medical symptom searches (Kaye, 2014). A study of over eighty thousand health-related web pages found that 90 per cent of them leaked user information to outside parties, including commercial data brokers (Libert, 2014). Sensitive medical conditions can become identifiable through the examination of other data sets, such as purchasing habits (Rosenblat, Wikelius, boyd, Pena Gangadharan, and Yu, 2014). Several researchers have demonstrated how easy it is to de-anonymise digital data about individuals using a small amount of additional information, often on the basis of patterns of behaviour or joined-up data sets that can then re-identify people (Singer, 2015).

Personal medical details are also very valuable to cyber-criminals. It has been estimated that the digital data black market is now more profitable than the illicit drug industry (Ablon, Libicki, and Golay, 2015). Data security is becoming increasingly more difficult to protect as 'smart' online objects connect with each other and share data, and as personal data are uploaded to cloud computing archives in increasingly large amounts (Barcena, Wueest, and Lau, 2014; Kitchin, 2014). Hackers can gain access to personal data at two key points: when these are being transmitted from one location to another, such as from a personal device to a cloud computing database; and when they are kept in databases (Barcena et al., 2014). If strong data encryption and authentication protocols are not employed, hackers are able to gain access to personal data more readily.

Cybercriminals are frequently targeting the American healthcare system for illegal access to details such as names of patients, diagnosis codes and health-insurance policy numbers. They then use these details to gain access to pharmaceuticals, to make fraudulent health-insurance claims or to sell the data themselves in the black market (Humer and Finkle, 2014). Hackers have already accessed the types of information that workplaces often request their employees to provide as part of wellness programs or health-insurance plans – for instance information on sexual activity, stress levels and mental health, drug consumption, preexisting medical conditions and blood-test information (Pettypiece, 2014). Private health information details have been subject to numerous privacy breaches. Since 2009 over one thousand incidents have been reported to the US Department of Health and Human Services, all related to the hacking of digitised health information that should have been protected by the Health Insurance Portability and Accountability Act (Pettypiece, 2014).

Many internet and mobile technology users face difficulties in understanding or accessing the terms and conditions of the software and hardware that they use (Nissenbaum, 2011; Rosenzweig, 2012; Tene and Polonetsky, 2013). Some self-trackers may be unconcerned that their personal information is being used for profit or managerial purposes by others, or may view this as a trade-off designed to secure their ability to use various devices or software. Sometimes users agree to the use of their personal data by third parties as an unavoidable part of accepting the terms and conditions of devices, apps and platforms, or customer loyalty schemes (although to what extent users actually read through the fine print on these documents is not known). In other cases the users' data may be accessed for the purposes of others without the users' knowledge or consent. However, in the wake of the publicity stirred around Edward Snowden's revelations about governments' surveillance of their citizens and extensive news coverage of the ways in which big data are being harvested for commercial purposes or illegally accessed by hackers, people are becoming more aware of how often they are digitally monitored by others. There is a growing sense that individuals are being placed under dataveillance without their knowledge or express consent (Crawford and Schultz, 2014; Hartzog and Selinger, 2013; Polonetsky and Tene, 2013; Wellcome Trust, 2013).

The mass media are replete with such statements as 'Google/Facebook/Amazon knows you better than you know yourself'. The argument is that the internet empires' capacity to collect routine transactional data on users and to apply their algorithms so as to interpret and predict their habits and preferences provides insights on features that users themselves may not have known they possessed. The implications for self-tracking practitioners have also been identified. For example, in an article for the technology website PandoDaily entitled 'You are your data: The scary future of the quantified self', the author speculates on the ways in which personal data may be used for surveillance by others – including credit card companies, insurers and employers:

> As we document and share more of where we go, what we do, who we spend time with, what we eat, what we buy, how hard we exert ourselves, and so on, we create more data that companies can and will use to evaluate our worthiness – or lack thereof – for their products, services, and opportunities. For those of us who don't measure up compared to the rest of the population, the outcome won't be pretty. (Carney, 2013)

The knowledge that the big data empires and security organisations appear to have about people often unsettle people (Wellcome Trust, 2013). Some find this apparent superior knowledge about themselves 'creepy' (Tene and Polonetsky, 2013). Many express powerlessness in the face of the authority that internet empires have to collect, own and harvest their personal data (Andrejevic, 2014; Andrejevic and Burdon, 2015).

A study carried out by the Pew Research Center in late 2014 (Pew Research Center, 2014) found that the Americans they surveyed were displaying caution about how their personal online interactions and data were being monitored by security agencies and commercial entities. Their respondents were concerned about their personal data security. Nearly all of them were aware of the implications of Snowden's revelations about how the government was monitoring their private online communications and expressed the belief that people had lost control over how their digitised personal information was collected and used by companies. The people surveyed demonstrated a universal lack of confidence in the security of online communication channels and were highly aware of the difficulty of preserving anonymity on the internet. The respondents viewed their social security numbers as the most sensitive piece of personal information that they wished to protect, and this was followed by their health and medical information as the next most sensitive category.

A Wellcome Trust study that conducted qualitative research with British people similarly found that many participants viewed health- and medical-related information differently from other kinds of data. Participants saw the collection and sharing of their own data – their medical records – across healthcare sites in a positive light, as beneficial to their own healthcare. However, they were less sanguine about these private data being shared outside the NHS (National Health Service) system, and especially with employers and private companies that may seek to profit from the data (Wellcome Trust, 2013). In their British study, Dennison, Morrison, Conway, and Yardley (2013) found that several participants expressed concern about the security of the personal data they uploaded onto self-tracking apps and about the ways in which third parties might use this information. They were particularly sensitive about the possibility that details about their mental or physical health might be used by commercial entities that intended to target them with advertisements or might be broadcast on social media sites without their permission.

Nafus (2014: 217) uses the evocative phrase 'data's capacity for betrayal' when discussing the unintended consequences of engaging in sensor-based self-monitoring. Her participants were using home energy-monitoring systems. Some of them were concerned about the possibility that criminals may hack into the data and recognise when a home's inhabitants are out and may steal people's possessions, or that energy companies may use people's detailed energy use data for their own purposes. This sense of betrayal was also evident in another study – of Australian families that used home energy monitors (Snow, Buys, Roe, and Brereton, 2013). One participant in this project recounted an incident in which her husband had been examining their home's energy use from his digital device at work. Her own energy use had been noted and remarked upon by an onlooker who knew the couple and went so far as to telephone her to comment on her energy use. She was confronted by this loss of privacy. A teenage girl described how her parents could monitor when she was using the air conditioning at home by reviewing the energy monitoring system data; this discomforted her and made her feel under their surveillance. Such experiences reveal how self-monitoring can easily slide into surveillance by others, who could be members of one's own family.

In response to these issues, privacy and human rights organisations have begun to call for legislation and bills of rights that promote greater transparency in the ways in which big data are used by second and third parties. Critics have contended that a new 'digital divide' is emerging, in which powerful institutions and organisations such as the internet empires have control over digital data while others are excluded from access (Andrejevic, 2013, 2014; boyd and Crawford, 2012).

In February 2015 the Nuffield Council on Bioethics published a report on the ethics of the collection and use of data in medical research and healthcare that refers to the personal data gathered voluntarily by people as part of self-tracking practices (such data are referred to in the report as 'patient-generated data'). The report's authors are strongly in favour of better control over the security and privacy of such information – so much so that they discuss drawing up a legal framework for dealing with these issues and imposing criminal penalties on the misuse of these types of data. They emphasise the importance of (1) developing ethical principles for the use of medical and healthcare data – principles that should be grounded in ideas of respect for persons, privacy and human rights; (2) incorporating the full range of values and interests of all actors involved; and (3) maintaining effective accountability in relation to data initiatives. Similarly, the Insight Ireland Centre for Data Analytics produced a white paper that set out a 'Magna Carta for big data' (Predict, 2015). The white paper's authors contend that the rights of all stakeholders – commercial bodies, the government and the public – need to be acknowledged by policy development. This entails protecting the privacy of the public appropriately while ensuring that government, research and commercial use of big data can still take place.

Apple's Tim Cook has taken a major stance by arguing that personal data and security are extremely important and should be protected. Apple's policy is that their product is the devices they sell, not the personal data that are generated by using the devices (Heath, 2015). For example, Apple announced in September 2014 that it was improving personal data encryption on its iPhones and iPads, following similar moves by Google and Yahoo. However, iPhone and iPad users are still encouraged to sign up to Apple's iCloud data-syncing and storage service, and the information and images that are stored there may be accessed by hackers or government security agencies. While these data on iCloud may also be encrypted by Apple, Apple uses its own password to encrypt them, and it may be forced to decrypt them at the government's request (M. Lee, 2014).

Communal self-tracking and taking control of personal data

What may be termed 'communal self-tracking' involves the consensual sharing of a tracker's personal data with other people, as a central feature of self-tracking practice. The people who take part in this process may use social media, platforms designed for comparing and sharing personal data, and sites such as the Quantified Self website, in order to engage with, and learn from, other self-trackers. Some people attend meetups or conferences in a desire to meet face to face with other self-trackers and share their data and evaluations of the different techniques and devices for self-tracking.

The Quantified Self website often refers to participants as engaging in a community and encourages the sharing of personal data with one another. Indeed an emphasis on this process as part of the ethos of the quantified self has been evident since the earliest days of the Quantified Self movement. In his first article on the quantified self for *Wired* magazine, Gary Wolf (2009) asserted that self-tracking involves the sharing of data and collaboration on ways of using them, and therefore it is not a 'particularly individual-istic' practice.

Self-trackers may share their data on the Quantified Self website or on other sites, on their own blogs or on social media sites such as Twitter, where the hashtag #quantifiedself is often employed to draw other self-trackers' attention to their posts. Some people choose to tell a very personal story, perhaps about how they used self-tracking in response to grief about the loss of a family member, or in response to their struggles with eating disorders, bowel problems or weight. As I noted in Chapter 4, this kind of sharing involves emo-tional disclosure to the group or online community. Others focus on how they use particular methods or devices and thus engage in a more technical exposition (Barta and Neff, 2014).

Notions of 'small data' and 'big data' are part of these discussions of how personal data may contribute to shared goals. There are various interpretations of what the term 'small data' means, which are inflected via the contexts in which the term is discussed. One definition that recurs in popular forums presents small data as information that indi-viduals, organisations or businesses collect on themselves of their own will and for their own purposes. Small data are defined as personal and identifiable; big data as impersonal and anonymous. Small data are often represented as more contextual and easy to manage, because there are fewer data points. Information that is deliberately collected by someone for oneself, as part of self-tracking initiatives, is often repre-sented as a form of small data.

Several commentators have begun to refer to 'the quantified us' as a way of articulating how the small data produced
by self-trackers may be usefully incorporated into large data
sets if one wants to 'get more meaning out of our data'
(Ramirez, 2013). As one account of 'the quantified us'
puts it:

> One of the ways we can transition the Quantified Self move-
> ment to have more impact, is to bridge the gap between Big
> and small data, and to heighten the collective relevance of the
> data we track about ourselves. By uncovering insights about
> ourselves through looking closely at others who are like us in
> the most meaningful ways, we can chart new paths toward
> becoming the people we want to be. (Jordan and Pfarr, 2014)

As this suggests, the concept of 'quantified us' still focuses
firmly on the individual's agenda. The idea is to draw on
others' pooled data to further one's own interests and goals:
'Quantified Self can provide added value, when you start
sharing your data online and other self-trackers share their
data as well. All this [sic] combined data provide an enor-
mous amount of extra information for you' (de Groot, 2014).
Therefore, while there is constant reference among members
of the Quantified Self movement to the 'quantified-self community', this community largely refers to sharing personal
data with one another or learning from others' data or from
self-tracking or data visualisation methods, so that one's own
data practices may be improved.

This perspective is also evident in the discourse of organisations such as the Small Data Lab, which are beginning to
be established in order to provide software and assist people
in harvesting their own data so that they can access 'the big
insights and meaning this small data contains [sic] within'
(Small Data Lab, 2014). In this initiative, the personal
by-product data that people contribute to big data sets are
reclaimed and returned to these individuals for their own use.
The ideal is to create a 'rich personal data ecology', in which
the various forms of data that people generate can be archived
and joined together in 'personal data vaults' to provide
insights for those users (Paz, 2013).

This drive towards 'sharing your numbers' and recounting
experiences of self-tracking fits into the wider discourse of

sharing personal details and experiences with others, which underpins many activities on Web 2.0 social media platforms (Beer and Burrows, 2013; John, 2013). In this discourse of sharing, help and support from others, and building better information from aggregated data sets, individualism as expressed in self-tracking cultures can have a strongly participatory dimension. Individualism remains a key attribute; but it is contended that one can achieve the optimal self more quickly as part of a participatory culture. Self-entrepreneurialism is represented both as contributing to the broader knowledges developed via digitisation and as benefiting from digitisation, in a synergistic or cybernetic relationship of self to others. In this context self-reinvention and reflexivity are shared undertakings.

The imperative of being able to manage and control the continuous streams of information that are generated by self-tracking is integral to self-tracking cultures, as I discussed in Chapter 4. Reflecting on the challenges of which data to collect, how to make sense of and visualise the data, and how to apply this knowledge to one's life is part of the issue of 'controlling my data', which frequently comes up for discussion on the Quantified Self website and in members' meetups and conferences. Increasingly, such discussions incorporate examination of how self-trackers' personal data are used by other actors and agencies and how the users themselves can seek to gain greater control over where the data go and how they are used.

Nafus and Sherman (2014: 1785) contend that self-tracking is an alternative data practice that is a form of soft resistance to algorithmic authority and to the harvesting of individuals' personal data. They argue that self-tracking is nothing less than 'a profoundly different way of knowing what data is, why it is important, who gets to interpret it [*sic*], and to what ends'. However the issue of gaining access to one's data remains crucial to questions of data control and use. While a small minority of technically proficient self-trackers are able to devise their own digital technologies for self-tracking and thus exert full control over their personal information, the vast majority must rely on the commercialised products that are available and therefore lose control over where their data are stored and who is able to gain access. For people who have chronic health conditions, for example, access to their data can be a crucial issue. A debate is continuing over the data that are collected by continuous blood glucose monitoring and whether the patients should have ready access to these data or only their doctors. As one person with diabetes contends on his blog, older self-care blood glucose-monitoring devices produce data that patients can view and act on immediately. Why should the information generated by the newer digitised continuous blood glucose monitors be available only to doctors, who review it some time later, when patients could benefit from seeing their data in real time (Dubois, 2014)? A similar issue arises in relation to the information that is collected on heart patients' defibrillator implants. The data that are conveyed wirelessly to patients' healthcare professionals cannot be easily accessed by the patients themselves. In jurisdictions such as the United States, the device developers are legally prohibited from allowing patients access to their data (Dockser Marcus and Weaver, 2012).

There is recent evidence that the Quantified Self movement is becoming more interested in facilitating access to personal data for purposes beyond those of individuals. In a post on the Quantified Self website entitled 'Access matters', Gary Wolf (2014) comments that self-trackers have no legal access to their own data, which they may have collected for years. Nor is there an informal ethical consensus that supports developers in opening their archives to the people who have contributed their information. Wolf and others associated with the Quantified Self movement have begun to campaign for self-trackers to achieve greater access to the personal data that are presently sequestered in the cloud computing archives of developers. They argue for an approach that leads to the aggregation of self-tracked data in ways that will benefit other people than individual self-trackers themselves.

Some Quantified Self movement-affiliated groups have begun to experiment with ways in which self-tracking can be used for community participation and development. Members of the St Louis Quantified Self meeting group, for example, have worked on developing a context-specific app that allows people to input their moods and identify how certain spatial locations within a community affect emotional responses. They are also developing a Personal Environment Tracker that would allow St Louis citizens to monitor their own environmental impact and that of the community in which they live (Ramirez, 2014).

The Quantified Self Lab, the technical arm of the Quantified Self movement, has also announced that it is becoming involved with citizen science initiatives in collaboration with the US Environmental Protection Agency (Ramirez, 2015). It has now joined with the Robert Wood Johnson Foundation, an American philanthropic organisation focused on health issues, to work on improving people's access to their personal data. Both groups are also collaborating with other partners on the Open Humans Network (Open Humans, 2015), which is aimed at facilitating the sharing of people's details about their health and medical statuses as part of a participatory research initiative. Participants who join in this initiative are asked to upload the data that they have collected on themselves through self-tracking devices as well as any other digitised information about their bodies that they are able to offer for use in research studies. Part of the model that the Open Humans Network has adopted is that researchers agree to return to the participants themselves any new data that emerge from projects that use these participants' information, and participants decide which of their data they allow others to access.

A number of initiatives have developed that incorporate the aggregation of self-tracked data with those of others (apart from members of the Quantified Self movement), as part of projects designed to benefit both the individuals who have collected the data and the broader community. Citizen science, environmental activism, healthy cities and community development projects are examples of these types of communal self-tracking endeavours. These initiatives, sometimes referred to as 'citizen sensing' (Gabrys, 2014), are a form of crowdsourcing. They may involve the use of data that individuals collect on their local environs, such as air quality, traffic levels or crime rates, as well as on their own health indicators – or a combination of both. These data may be used in various ways. Sometimes they are simply part of collective projects undertaken at the behest of local agencies, but they may also be used in political efforts to challenge governmental policy and agitate for improved services or planning. The impetus may come from grassroots organisations or from governmental organisations; the latter construe it as a top-down initiative or as an encouragement towards community development.

Self-tracked data here become represented as a tool for promoting personal health and wellbeing at the same time as community and environmental development and sustainability. As these initiatives suggest, part of the ethical practice of self-tracking, at least for some practitioners, may involve the notion of contributing to a wider good as well as collecting data for one's own purposes. Access to large data sets – rendering these data sets more 'open' and accessible to members of the public – becomes a mode of citizenship that is distributed between self, community and physical environment. This idea extends the entrepreneurial and responsible citizen ideal by incorporating expectations that people should not only collect their own, personal information for purposes of self-optimisation but should also contribute it to tailored, aggregated big data that will benefit many others, in a form of personal data philanthropy: self-tracking citizenship, in other words.

Responses and resistances to dataveillance

As humans increasingly become nodes in the Internet of Things, generating and exchanging digital data with other sensor-equipped objects, self-tracking practices, whether taken up voluntarily or pushed or imposed upon people, will become unavoidable for many. The evidence outlined in this book suggests a gradually widening scope for the use of self-tracking, which is likely to expand as a growing number of agencies and organisations realise the potential of the data produced from these practices. As the monitoring of individuals' bodies, energy use, work productivity, moods, social relationships, purchasing habits, driving practices and so on becomes more routine and widespread, the extent to which the subjects of this tracking can opt out becomes limited. People may have few choices about whether or not to participate as data-generating subjects.

It is important, however, to emphasise that dataveillance (or any other mode of watching) is not an inevitable, fail-safe operation. It is always responded to with resistant strategies (Raley, 2013) that may be more or less effective. While people can no longer escape being the subjects of dataveillance, they can to some extent make choices about the self-tracking practices in which they may engage and about the devices they decide to use. They may seek out developers and manufacturers who are responding to consumers' concerns about data privacy and security.

There have also been calls for the use of the policy of 'privacy by design' when developing digital devices. This concept emphasises that the protection of consumers' privacy should be a major element in the design of objects such as smart technologies. Such discussions refer to the notions of the 'user-centric internet' and 'controlled computing', where people's personal data will be protected by the judicious structuring of information systems engineering, above the demands of those who wish to profit from or otherwise use these data (Cavoukian and Kruger, 2014). As a designer of digital systems, Lloyd (2014) argues for the importance of making systems that are more transparent, so that users can understand how they operate, what information they are collecting and how these data are algorithmically interpreted. She advocates for digital systems that give over more agency to users, so that they feel more in control.

Dodge and Kitchin (Dodge and Kitchin, 2007; Kitchin and Dodge, 2011) have suggested that lifeloggers should not try to achieve the total recording of as many details of their lives as they can, as is proposed by the ideal of lifelogging. Instead, as a way of evading surveillance and the appropriation of their personal details by others, lifeloggers should seek to achieve only a partial record, by using devices that block the recording of some details or record others only imperfectly. Dodge and Kitchin (2007) also suggest that 'an ethics of forgetting' should be incorporated into the design of lifelogging devices and software as part of allowing people to forget some aspects of their lives and to evade the close surveillance of their lives exerted by others. People should be able to 'dupe the log' in order to 'unsettle the authenticity of the record' (Dodge and Kitchin, 2007: 439).

Dodge and Kitchin (2007) further assert that forgetting should be viewed as an emancipatory process, which allows for the freedom of escaping the bounds of remembering, rather than as a weakness or fallibility, as lifelogging discourses tend to suggest. The best type of lifelog, they argue, is one that conforms to the fallibility of human memory so that it might degrade in terms of its accuracy over time, as human memory does, losing or changing some details while preserving others. The recording of an event, for example, would be an impression rather than a highly precise and accurate record. Algorithmic strategies could be incorporated into digital self-tracking devices in order to promote this type of duping of the log and to evade the 'merciless memory' of digital recording of details (Dodge and Kitchin, 2007: 443).

Various other strategies for dealing with a perceived loss of control over people's personal data have been proposed. One is that of obfuscation: the deliberate production of false, misleading or ambiguous data (Brunton and Nissenbaum, 2011). Examples of software that has been developed for this purpose include AdNauseam and TrackMeNot. These are browser extensions that have been expressly designed as political strategies for online users to avoid dataveillance by commercial companies. They do not use encryption or concealment, but instead the opposing strategies of creating digital 'noise'. TrackMeNot hides real web searches among a plethora of false ones, creating 'ghost queries'. AdNauseam works in conjunction with an ad-blocker tool. It automatically clicks on blocked ads that the user has never viewed, thus creating a false trail of information about the users' browsing habits and rendering user profiling and monitoring useless for the ad networks' databases.

Other means of engaging in counterveillance include the use of such tools as Eyebrowse, a Firefox plug-in that visualises the user's web browsing history as well as those of the user's friends. In so doing, this tool displays the data that internet companies are able to collect when people browse the internet. The use of this type of tool may be described as a self-tracking technology for revealing others' tracking of a person's activities (in other words, the tracking of tracking), with the objective of developing greater awareness of where people's personal information goes when it enters the digital data economy. Here self-tracking becomes a mode of learning about a user's participation as a subject in dataveillance.

Final Reflections

I have suggested in this book that self-tracking cultures have emerged in a sociocultural and political context in which various rationales, discourses, practices and technologies are converging. These include the following:

- concepts of the self that value self-knowledge and self-entrepreneurialism;
- ideas about the body that champion tight regulation, control and order;
- the privileging of knowledges that are regarded as scientific, and therefore neutral and objective, supposedly unsullied by human subjectivity or bias;
- a moral and political environment in which taking responsibility for one's life and health is privileged and promoted;
- the affordances of new digital technologies that are able to monitor an increasing array of aspects of human bodies, behaviours, preferences and habits in ever greater detail;
- the emergence of the digital data knowledge economy, in which digitised personal information bears significant commercial, managerial and research value; and
- the realisation, on the part of governmental, managerial and commercial actors and agencies, that they can

mobilise for their own purposes the data derived from
self-tracking.

The notion of autonomous individualism is articulated in
many accounts of self-tracking practices. Even when a communal approach to self-tracking is adopted, forums that
discuss reflexive self-monitoring often show little recognition
of or interest in the fact that the self is always inevitably sited
within social, cultural and political contexts; that people are
always part of social groups and acculturated into specific
cultural norms; and that their bodies are always experienced
in relation to others' bodies. Instead selves and bodies are
understood as atomised, shaped by personal life experiences
and empowered to manipulate their destinies by acquiring
self-knowledge and acting rationally upon this knowledge.

Self-tracking technologies, discourses and practices predominantly assume a certain type of user, located within a
supportive economic and social milieu. They tend not to
acknowledge or recognise the effects of low income or poverty,
racism, sexism, living with a mental health condition or a
disability, residing in a remote community, identifying as
queer or transgender or belonging to an ethnic or racial
minority group. Life success, wellbeing, productivity and
good health are portrayed as the outcomes of individuals'
work upon themselves. This user is privileged, autonomous,
willing and able to conform to the dictates associated with
the notion of a self-responsible actor. The contradictions,
apparent irrationalities and ambivalences that are part of
most people's life experience are elided, as are the vagaries of
fate and the social determinants of living conditions.

As I have remarked in this book's chapters, via the mainstream self-tracking devices and software that are available,
certain aspects of selfhood and embodiment are selected for
monitoring while a plethora of others are inevitably left out,
ignored, or not even considered in the first place. Those
aspects that are selected become more visible, while others
are obscured or neglected through this process. The technologies themselves, including the mobile, wearable and 'anti-
wearable' sensor-embedded objects and the software that
animate them, tend to be the product of a narrow demographic of designers: white, well-paid, heterosexual men

living in the Global North. In consequence, the tacit assumptions and norms that underpin the design and affordances of self-tracking technologies are shaped by these people's decisions, preferences and values. Thus, for example, devices such as Apple Watch initially failed to include a menstrual cycle tracker as part of its built-in features (Eveleth, 2014); sexuality self-tracking apps focus on male sexual performance and competitive displays of prowess (Lupton, 2015c); apps that use westernised concepts and images of health and the human body are inappropriate for Aboriginal people living in remote areas of Australia (Christie and Verran, 2014). How people from outside this demographic might engage or not with these technologies and how technologies might be better designed to acknowledge the diversity of socioeconomic advantage, cultures and sexual identities are subjects rarely pondered upon in the world of technology design.

In one of the very few culturally and politically reflexive accounts of developing an app, design anthropologist Bryce Peake (2015) writes about her attempts to 'decolonise' app design by challenging the westernised and privileged perspective that is typical of mainstream apps. She worked on developing a self-tracking app for people living with tinnitus who belonged to underprivileged nonwhite ethnic and racial groups in the city of Portland, Oregon. Peake notes the concern that some of her collaborators expressed about being monitored by the government via their own use of such apps: their nonlegal status as immigrants would then be discovered. A woman of African American and Native American descent expressed a worry about the fact that, for generations, white people (including anthropologists) had collected data on her ancestors, as part of paternalistic and subjugating ideologies. Hence she was ambivalent about becoming imbricated in yet another surveillance endeavour led by white people. Such concerns led Peake to design the app in ways that sought to incorporate the users' cultural worldviews and to protect the privacy and security of their personal data, so that they had greater control over them.

At the same time as self-tracking practices are reductive and selective, they are also productive. They bring into being new knowledges, assemblages, subjectivities and forms of embodiment and social relations. In Chapter 2 I referred to the four types of technology identified by Foucault, which work together to produce knowledges on humans. Acts of reflexive self-monitoring involve all four of these knowledge technologies. Via prosumption, self-trackers generate data on themselves (technologies of production); they manipulate and communicate the symbols, images, discourses and ideas related to their own data and the devices that generate these data (technologies of sign systems); they are involved in strategies that are designed to assist them in participating in certain forms of conduct for specific ends (technologies of power); and all of these practices are overtly and deliberately directed at performing, presenting and improving the self (technologies of the self).

What is particularly intriguing about this expertise is that it both operates at the level of the 'nonexpert' (the self-tracker), where it is configured, and is inextricably inter-bound into the digital data economy and the forms of government regulation of the body politic. The authority of the knowledgeable expert on human life is dispersed among members of the lay public to a greater extent than ever before. However, the shared nature of this authority and expertise also undermines the power that self-trackers possess over their own information. Reflexive self-monitors are able to generate their own truth claims about trackers' own bodies/selves, but these trackers are increasingly unable to control how these truth claims are used by other actors or what the potential ramifications for their own life chances and opportunities are once these data come under the control of others.

In recent times there have been arguments, occasionally put forward by commentators in news items or blog posts, that self-tracking devices have not achieved the success and consumer take-up that were expected of them a few years ago. Such commentators point to statistics that suggest that not as many fitness trackers have been sold as expected, that those who buy them tend to use them only for a short time and that the information these trackers generate is obvious or too difficult to act upon (see, for example, Carney, 2015). This may well be the case with certain types of fitness track-ers, on which such articles usually centre. As I have shown in this book, however, self-tracking can no longer be viewed purely as an individual enterprise, limited to those people who decide that they want to count the number of steps they take, the calories they ingest or the hours they sleep each night by using an app or a wearable device. These practices represent only a small element in the new self-tracking cultures and practices. Self-tracking has been taken up in various social domains, for objectives that go well beyond the individual's quest for self-knowledge and self-improvement on the basis of personal goals, and well beyond fitness and health tracking.

I have identified five modes of tracking: private (confined to individuals' consensual and personal objectives), pushed (where the initiative for self-tracking comes from an external agent), communal (which involves sharing personal information with others), imposed (which involves the imposition of self-tracking practices upon individuals by other actors and agencies) and exploited (where people's personal data are used or repurposed for the managerial, research or commercial benefit of others). There are intersections and recursive relationships between all of these self-tracking modes, but there are also observable differences related to (1) the extent to which self-tracking is taken up by consent; and (2) the purposes to which the data thus created are put.

The idea of smart objects exchanging information with one another and learning from one another leads to a new way of thinking about humans' relationships with their machines. Digital devices are learning more about humans as they create data assemblages in endless intertwinings and new configurations of data. Data are exchanged between objects and humans, in networks of data generation and sharing that offer myriads of inexhaustible potentialities of data assemblages. Commentators contributing to discussions of the coming Internet of Things have argued that, as sensor-embedded technologies become increasingly pervasive in the built environment and in wearable technologies and as software such as apps become anticipatory and automatic rather than requiring human intervention in order to be run, we are moving towards a digitised environment that is responsive and unobtrusive to the point that the computer interface recedes into the background (Elwell, 2014; Greengard, 2015).

It is intriguing to speculate about how the growing Internet of Things/Internet of Life will begin to influence and facilitate self-tracking practices and cultures. We have already reached a point where smart objects and apps tell us what to do and nudge or even nag us on the basis of the self-tracked data they have generated from us. The smart objects that already exist – such as clothes, jewellery and watches that can measure bodily functions and movements, cars that can monitor driving habits, fridges that notice if the milk is almost gone and home thermostat systems that know when their inhabitants are likely to wake up in the morning – may potentially be joined by tables that can listen to and understand the conversations of people meeting around them, chairs that measure how long a person sits in them, kitchen chopping boards that record food preparation habits, sofas that eject people who have been sitting in them too long and 3D printers that prepare certain types of food for people on the basis of their bodily activity data for that day. While such uses of personal data may make life more convenient in many instances, the ever growing plethora of data assemblages that are configured and the constant exchange of data between smart objects raise important questions about human agency and dependency on technologies, data security and privacy, and the control and use of information about individuals.

Discussions of 'data literacy' that describe the understandings and practices of digital technology users are beginning to appear in public and academic forums. Such discussions often fail to acknowledge the political dimensions of data literacies. People's willing participation in generating information about themselves can be rewarding and beneficial for their own purposes, as I have discussed in previous chapters. Beer (2013: 109) uses the concept of 'data play' to describe the creative, pleasurable and productive ways in which prosumers create, use, visualise and share their own digital data. Many self-trackers may be viewed as engaging in a form of data play. However, both the extent to which people fully understand how their data are being used by second and third parties and the proliferating ways in which these data may be stolen by hackers, accessed by governmental security agencies or used to discriminate against their owners or limit their opportunities require continued detailed and critical examination. It is important to bring together concepts of data politics and data literacies in order to focus attention (1) on the power relations that underpin digital design and market-ing – not only from the perspective of users but also from the position of technology designers and developers; and (2) on the commercial and governmental agencies that are using and exploiting personal data.

How might self-tracking be used in ways that go beyond the current focus on individualisation, self-optimisation and the expropriation and exploitation of people's personal infor-mation by second and third parties? One avenue of possibility is demonstrated in the '20 Day Stranger' project established at the Dalai Lama Center for Ethics and Transformative Values at the MIT (MIT Media Lab Playful Systems, 2014). This project seeks to promote the exchange of personal data with strangers as a means of sharing 'one person's experience of the world with another's'. Participants use an iPhone app and for a period of 20 days share with the anonymous others the data that the phone generates about themselves, including photographs, geolocation details and body metrics. This kind of project is directed at developing empathy and understanding of others' lives – goals that are worthwhile in themselves and challenge the solipsism of dominant modes of self-tracking.

The ways in which self-trackers collect, manage, negotiate and interpret personal data offer insights that have broader implications for other data practices in contemporary digital society. Given the mounting interest in the role played by the researcher as an embodied and sensual being in the research process, some of the findings of this book also offer intriguing reflections on research practice. The relationships between the immaterial and the material, between digital and nondigi-tal, qualitative and quantitative data, and between experience (individual or collective) and the ways in which knowledges are configured, communicated and interpreted are all called into question by self-tracking practices and cultures. Self-tracking offers some perspectives on sense making and iden-tity formation that have broader relevance.

There is much more to explore in this realm of investiga-tion, which seeks to examine the 'sensory aesthetics' (Pink and Leder Mackley, 2014) of reflexive self-monitoring. Using the kind of sensory digital ethnography outlined by cultural researchers such as Sarah Pink and her colleagues (Pink,

2009; Pink and Leder Mackley, 2013, 2014), these often unacknowledged elements of self-monitoring in everyday life might be further investigated. In seeking to provide insights into one's life and on oneself, for example, people may be confronted with a particular odour or taste and ask themselves what it is about these phenomena that attracts or repels them. How do they elicit memories and concepts of social encounters and social ties, and how do these relate to their sense of self and the ways in which they conduct their lives? Such sensuous ways of knowing (Low, 2013) go beyond the sanitised, desensitised world of standard digital information about people and potentially provide far deeper and richer insights into selves and bodies.

I referred in Chapter 5 to artistic and design interventions that approach self-tracking from different perspectives from those offered by dominant representations. These approaches attempt to situate design, engineering and art making within their broader social and political contexts, serving to challenge social inequalities and to provoke resistance and critical reflection (Ratto, Wylie, and Jalbert, 2014). Such endeavours can contribute much to a critical sociocultural analysis of the concerns at stake in the contemporary world of dataveillance and to the growing dispersal of modes of self-tracking and of the multiple actors and agencies that now enjoin the practice on people and seek to use the data that are generated. These interventions can not only reveal the emotional resonances of these practices, the pleasures and anxieties that underlie them, but also imagine new possibilities and transformations of the present.

Such a re-imagining of the possibilities of self-tracking practices goes well beyond the standard focus on self-improvement and self-management or exploitation of personal data that characterises self-tracking cultures. These types of projects will become increasingly important, as people are increasingly required to engage in self-tracking at the behest of others. There are opportunities for using self-tracking technologies in ways that are more overtly political and seek to challenge the status quo. Outside the work of artists and the use of sensor-based technologies for activist initiatives in citizen science, we have yet to witness sustained efforts to engage in self-tracking as a strategic and political bodily intervention. Yet the capacity to approach self-tracking in this way offers many intriguing possibilities to those who seek to challenge tacit assumptions and stereotypes about bodies and selves. There are opportunities for self-generated information to configure new norms of selfhood and embodiment, which challenge or resist the dominant norms that conventional self-tracking technologies and practices tend to support, reproduce and configure.

Here the cyborg politics of Donna Haraway (1991) might be brought to bear if one wishes to think through the way in which self-tracking can be transformed into a political act. In her work, Haraway emphasises the complex, dynamic, unstable and often unpredictable nature of any human–technology intertwining and the potential for political disruption and challenges that this brings with it. If we can get beyond fixed assumptions about what bodies/selves are or should be and confront taken-for-granted norms that assume that certain types of people are inferior or lacking, then the possibility for social change may be imagined. Self-tracked data could be employed to produce compelling information that would challenge negative or confining assumptions and norms; or they could be used as a form of citizen hactivism, in the service of agitating for social change and acknowledging the social determinants of health, productivity and wellbeing.

References

2014 QS Europe Conference (2014): Show & tell talks. http://quantifiedself.com/2014/04/2014-qs-europe-conference-showtell-talks (accessed 16 June 2014).

Ablon, L., Libicki, M., and Golay, A. (2015) *Markets for Cybercrime Tools and Stolen Data*. Santa Monica, CA: RAND Corporation.

Ackerman, L. (2013) *Mobile Health and Fitness Applications and Information Privacy*. San Diego, CA: Privacy Rights Clearing House.

Adkins, L. and Lury, C. (2011) Introduction: Special measures. *The Sociological Review*, 59 (s2): 5–23.

Agapakis, C. and Tolaas, S. (2014) Selfmade: Installation, 2013. Trinity College Dublin Science Gallery. https://dublin.sciencegallery.com/growyourown/selfmade (accessed 20 March 2015).

Ajana, B. (2013) *Governing through Biometrics: The Biopolitics of Identity*. Basingstoke: Palgrave Macmillan.

Albrechtslund, A. and Lauritsen, P. (2013) Spaces of everyday surveillance: Unfolding an analytical concept of participation. *Geoforum*, 49: 310–16.

Allen, A. L. (2008) Dredging up the past: Lifelogging, memory, and surveillance. *The University of Chicago Law Review*, 75 (1): 47–74.

Amoore, L. (2011) Data derivatives: On the emergence of a security risk calculus for our times, *Theory, Culture & Society*, 28 (6), 24–43.

Andersen, J. H. and Whyte, S. R. (2014) Measuring risk, managing values: Health technology and subjectivity in Denmark. *Anthropology & Medicine*, 21 (3): 265–76.

Andrejevic, M. (2013) *Infoglut: How Too Much Information Is Changing the Way We Think and Know*. New York: Routledge.

Andrejevic, M. (2014) The big data divide. *International Journal of Communication*, 8: 1673–89.

Andrejevic, M. and Burdon, M. (2015) Defining the sensor society. *Television & New Media*, 16 (1): 19–36.

Anonymous (2014) Kicking tracking, no picnic. The Unquantified Self. http://unquantifiedself.wordpress.com/2014/04/29/kicking -tracking-no-picnic (accessed 6 August 2014).

Appelboom, G., LoPresti, M., Reginster, J.-Y., Sander Connolly, E., and Dumont, E. P. L. (2014) The quantified patient: A patient participatory culture. *Current Medical Research and Opinion*, 30 (12): 2585–7.

Apple (2014) Apple Watch. https://www.apple.com/watch/ technology (accessed 6 October 2014).

Apple Store Nike Fuelband (2015) http://store.apple.com/us/ product/HE387VC/A/nike-fuelband-se-small?fnode=4a (accessed 17 February 2015; no current url).

Aslinger, B. and Huntemann, N. (2013) Digital media studies futures. *Media, Culture & Society*, 35 (1): 9–12.

Barcena, M. B., Wueest, C., and Lau, H. (2014) *How Safe Is Your Quantified Self?* Mountain View, CA: Symantech.

Barrass, S. (2014) Acoustic sonification of blood pressure in the form of a singing bowl. Paper presented at Conference on Sonification of Health and Environmental Data, York, UK, September.

Barta, K. and Neff, G. (2014) Technologies for sharing: Lessons from the Quantified Self movement about the political economy of platforms. Paper presented at the International Communication Association Conference, Seattle, Washington.

Bauman, Z. (2000) *Liquid Modernity*. Cambridge: Polity.

Beck, U. (1992) *Risk Society: Towards a New Modernity*. London: Sage.

Beck, U. (1999) *World Risk Society*. Malden, MA: Polity.

Beck, U. and Beck-Gernsheim, E. (1995) *The Normal Chaos of Love*. Cambridge: Polity.

Beer, D. (2009) Power through the algorithm? Participatory web cultures and the technological unconscious. *New Media & Society*, 11 (6): 985–1002.

Beer, D. (2013) *Popular Culture and New Media: The Politics of Circulation*. Basingstoke: Palgrave Macmillan.

Beer, D. and Burrows, R. (2013) Popular culture, digital archives and the new social life of data. *Theory, Culture & Society*, 30 (4): 47–71.

Bell, G. (2004) Intimate computing? *IEEE Internet Computing*, 8 (6): 91–93.

Bennett, C. J. (2011) In defence of privacy: The concept and the regime. *Surveillance & Society*, 8 (4): 485–96.

Best, K. (2010) Living in the control society: Surveillance, users and digital screen technologies. *International Journal of Cultural Studies*, 13 (1): 5–24.

Bijker, W., Hughes, T., Pinch, T., and Douglas, D. (2012) *The Social Construction of Technological Systems: New Directions in the Sociology and History of Technology*. Boston, MA: MIT Press.

Blumtritt, J. (2014) Organizing a system of 10 billion people. Datarella. http://datarella.com/organizing-a-system-of-10-billion -people (accessed 10 May 2014).

Boam, E. and Webb, J. (2014) The qualified self: Going beyond quantification. Design Mind. http://designmind.frogdesign.com/ articles/the-qualified-self-going-beyond-quantification.html (accessed 28 July 2014).

Boesel, W. E. (2013) Cyborgology: Return of the quantrepreneurs. The Society Pages. http://thesocietypages.org/cyborgology/2013/ 09/26/return-of-the-quantrepreneurs (accessed 1 August 2014).

Bossewitch, J. and Sinnreich, A. (2013) The end of forgetting: Strategic agency beyond the panopticon. *New Media & Society*, 15 (2): 224–42.

boyd, d. (2008) Facebook's privacy trainwreck: Exposure, invasion, and social convergence. *Convergence*, 14 (1): 13–20.

boyd, d. (2012) Networked privacy. *Surveillance & Society*, 10 (3/4): 348–50.

boyd, d. and Crawford, K. (2012) Critical questions for big data: Provocations for a cultural, technological, and scholarly phenomenon. *Information, Communication & Society*, 15 (5): 662–79.

Brandt, A. and Rozin, P. (1997) Introduction. In A. Brandt and P. Rozin, eds, *Morality and Health*, 1–11. New York: Routledge.

Brunton, F. and Nissenbaum, H. (2011) Vernacular resistance to data collection and analysis: A political theory of obfuscation. *First Monday*, 16 (5). http://firstmonday.org/ojs/index.php/fm/ article/view/3493 (accessed 16 October 2014).

Bucher, T. (2012) Want to be on the top? Algorithmic power and the threat of invisibility on Facebook. *New Media & Society*, 14 (7): 1164–80.

Burchell, G., Gordon, C., and Miller, P., eds. (1991) *The Foucault Effect: Studies in Governmentality*. Chicago, IL: University of Chicago Press.

Burrows, R. (2012) Living with the h-index? Metric assemblages in the contemporary academy. *The Sociological Review*, 60 (2): 355–72.

Carmichael, A. (2010) Why I stopped tracking. Quantified Self. http://quantifiedself.com/2010/04/why-i-stopped-tracking (accessed 22 April 2015).

Carney, M. (2013) You are your data: The scary future of the quantified self movement, PandoDaily. http://pando.com/2013/05/ 20/you-are-your-data-the-scary-future-of-the-quantified-self -movement (accessed 27 June 2014).

Carney, M. (2015) A decade in, the 'quantified self' is still more hope than reality. PandoDaily. http://pando.com/2015/03/20/ the-state-of-wearables (accessed 21 March 2015).

Cartwright, L. (1995) *Screening the Body: Tracing Medicine's Visual Culture*. Minneapolis, MN: University of Minnesota Press.

Castells, M. (2000) *The Rise of the Network Society*. Malden, MA: Blackwell.

Cavoukian, A. and Kruger, D. (2014) *Freedom and Control: Engineering a New Paradigm for the Digital World*. Privacy by Design. https://www.privacybydesign.ca/content/uploads/2014/05/pbd -freedom_control-Absio.pdf (accessed 25 September2015).

Cheney-Lippold, J. (2011) A new algorithmic identity: Soft biopolitics and the modulation of control. *Theory, Culture & Society*, 28 (6): 164–81.

Choe, E. K., Lee, N. B., Lee, B., Pratt, W., and Kientz, J. A. (2014) Understanding quantified-selfers' practices in collecting and exploring personal data. In *Proceedings of the Thirty-second Annual ACM Conference on Human Factors in Computing Systems*, 1143–52. Toronto: ACM.

Christie, M. and Verran, H. (2014) The Touch Pad body: A generative transcultural digital device interrupting received ideas and practices in Aboriginal health. *Societies*, 4 (2): 256–64. http:// www.mdpi.com/2075–4698/4/2/256 (accessed 11 July 2014).

Chrysanthou, M. (2002) Transparency and selfhood: Utopia and the informed body. *Social Science & Medicine*, 54 (3): 469–79.

Colt, S. (2014) Tim Cook gave his most in-depth interview to date: Here's what he said. Business Insider Australia. http://www .businessinsider.com.au/tim-cook-full-interview-with-charlie -rose-with-transcript-2014–9 (accessed 29 September 2014).

Comstock, J. (2014) Halamka: Time is right for patient-generated data, care traffic controllers needed. Mobi Health News. http:// mobihealthnews.com/35342/halamka-time-is-right-for-patient -generated-data-care-traffic-controllers-needed/?utm_source =hootsuite&utm_campaign=hootsuite (accessed 1 August 2014).

Coole, D. H. and Frost, S. (2010) *New Materialisms: Ontology, Agency, and Politics.* Durham, NC: Duke University Press.

Coughlin, J. (2014) What health and finance can learn from the quantified self and each other. The Huffington Post. http://www.huffingtonpost.com/joseph-f-coughlin/what-health-finance-can-learn-from-each-other_b_5774810.html (accessed 4 November 2014).

Crawford, K. and Schultz, J. (2014) Big data and due process: Toward a framework to redress predictive privacy harms. *Boston College Law Review*, 55 (1): 93–128.

Crawshaw, P. (2012) Governing at a distance: Social marketing and the (bio)politics of responsibility. *Social Science & Medicine*, 74 (1): 200–7.

Czerski, P. (2012) We, the web kids. *The Atlantic.* http://www.theatlantic.com/technology/archive/2012/02/we-the-web-kids/253382 (accessed 23 January 2015).

Darmour, J. (2013) 3 ways to make wearable tech actually wearable. Co.Design. http://www.fastcodesign.com/1672107/3-ways-to-make-wearable-tech-actually-wearable (accessed 15 March 2013).

Datta, A., Tschantz, M. C., and Datta, A. (2015) Automated experiments on ad privacy settings: A tale of opacity, choice, and discrimination. arXiv.org. http://arxiv.org/abs/1408.6491 (accessed 23 April 2015).

Davis, J. (2012) Social media and experiential ambivalence. *Future Internet*, 4 (4): 955–70.

Davis, J. (2013) The qualified self. Cyborgology. http://thesocietypages.org/cyborgology/2013/03/13/the-qualified-self (accessed 11 August 2013).

A Day in the Life (2014) A day in the life. http://deweyhagborg.com/day_in_the_life (accessed 11 November 2014).

Day, S., Lury, C., and Wakeford, N. (2014) Number ecologies: Numbers and numbering practices. *Distinktion: Scandinavian Journal of Social Theory*, 15 (2): 123–54.

de Groot, M. (2014) Quantified self, quantified us, quantified other. Quantified Self Institute. http://www.qsinstitute.org/?p=2048 (accessed 12 June 2014).

Dear Data (2015) Analog data-drawing project by Giorgia Lupi and Stefanie Posavec. http://www.dear-data.com/about (accessed 1 April 2015).

Dennison, L., Morrison, L., Conway, G., and Yardley, L. (2013) Opportunities and challenges for smartphone applications in supporting health behavior change: Qualitative study. *Journal of Medical Internet Research*, 15 (4): e86. http://www.jmir.org/2013/4/e86 (accessed 8 April 2014).

Deuze, M. (2011) Media life. *Media, Culture & Society*, 33 (1): 137–48.

Dewey-Hagborg, H. (2015) Stranger Visions: Sculpture, 2013. Trinity College Dublin Science Gallery. https://dublin.sciencegallery.com/growyourown/strangervisions (accessed 20 March 2015).

Dockser Marcus, A. and Weaver, C. (2012) Heart gadgets test privacy-law limits. *The Wall Street Journal*, 28 November. http://www.wsj.com/articles/SB10001424052970203937004578078820874744076 (accessed 8 April 2015).

Dodge, M. and Kitchin, R. (2007) 'Outlines of a world coming into existence': Pervasive computing and the ethics of forgetting. *Environment and Planning B: Planning and Design*, 34 (3): 431–45.

Douglas, M. (1966) *Purity and Danger: An Analysis of Concepts of Pollution and Taboo*. London: Routledge & Kegan Paul.

Dubois, W. (2014) Have professional CGMs passed their prime? Diabetes Mine. http://www.diabetesmine.com/2014/07/have-professional-cgms-passed-their-prime.html (accessed 29 July 2014).

Duden, B. (1993) *Disembodying Women: Perspectives on Pregnancy and the Unborn*, trans. L. Hoinacki. Cambridge, MA: Harvard University Press.

Duffy, J. (2014) 55 apps that can make you more productive. *PC Magazine*. http://www.pcmag.com/article2/0,2817,2395938,00.asp (accessed 22 June 2014).

Dunne, A. and Raby, F. (2013) *Speculative Everything: Design, Fiction, and Social Dreaming*. Cambridge, MA: MIT Press.

Ellerbrok, A. (2011) Playful biometrics: Controversial technology through the lens of play. *The Sociological Quarterly*, 52 (4): 528–47.

Elliott, A. (2013a) *Reinvention*. London: Routledge.

Elliott, A. (2013b) The theory of new individualism. In R. Tafarodi, ed., *Subjectivity in the Twenty-First Century: Psychological, Sociological, and Political Perspectives*, 190–209. Cambridge: Cambridge University Press.

Elmhurst Art Museum (2014) LifeLoggers: Chronicling the Everyday. https://www.elmhurstartmuseum.org/exhibitions/lifeloggers-chronicling-everyday (accessed 21 June 2014).

Elwell, J. S. (2014) The transmediated self: Life between the digital and the analog. *Convergence: The International Journal of Research into New Media Technologies*, 20 (2): 233–49.

Espeland, W. N. and Stevens, M. L. (1998) Commensuration as a social process. *Annual Review of Sociology*, 24: 313–43.

Esposti, S. D. (2014) When big data meets dataveillance: The hidden side of analytics. *Surveillance & Society*, 12 (2): 209–25.

Eveleth, R. (2014) How self-tracking apps exclude women. *The Atlantic*. http://www.theatlantic.com/technology/archive/2014/12/how-self-tracking-apps-exclude-women/383673 (accessed 16 December 2014).

Feehan, N. (2014) Social wearables. http://blog.nytlabs.com/2014/07/01/social-wearables (accessed 27 July 2014).

Feiler, B. (2014) The united states of metrics. *The New York Times*, 16 May. http://www.nytimes.com/2014/05/18/fashion/the-united-states-of-metrics.html?_r=3 (accessed 16 June 2014).

Feltron.com (2015) Nicholas Felton. http://feltron.com (accessed 11 April 2015).

Floating Data (2015) Laurie Frick. http://www.lauriefrick.com/floating-data (accessed 11 April 2015).

Foucault, M. (1977) *Discipline and Punish: The Birth of the Prison*. London: Penguin.

Foucault, M. (1979) *The History of Sexuality: An Introduction*. London: Penguin.

Foucault, M. (1984) The politics of health in the eighteenth century. In P. Rabinow, ed., *The Foucault Reader*, 273–89. New York: Pantheon.

Foucault, M. (1986) *The Care of the Self: The History of Sexuality*, vol. 3. New York: Pantheon.

Foucault, M. (1988) Technologies of the self. In L. Martin, H. Gutman, and P. Hutton, eds, *Technologies of the Self: A Seminar with Michel Foucault*, 16–49. London: Tavistock.

Foucault, M. (1991) Governmentality. In G. Burchell, C. Gordon, and P. Miller, eds, *The Foucault Effect: Studies in Governmentality*, 87–104. Hemel Hempstead: Harvester Wheatsheaf.

Fox, S. and Duggan, M. (2013) *Tracking for Health*. Washington, DC: Pew Research Center.

Frick, L. (2015) FRICKbits Data Art. https://itunes.apple.com/us/app/frickbits-data-art/id926472692?mt=8 (accessed 11 April 2015).

Frigo, A. (2015) 2004–2040. http://2004-2040.com (accessed 23 January 2015).

Fuchs, C. and Dyer-Witheford, N. (2013) Karl Marx @ Internet Studies. *New Media & Society*, 15 (5): 782–96.

Gabrys, J. (2014) Programming environments: Environmentality and citizen sensing in the smart city. *Environment and Planning D: Society and Space*, 32 (1): 30–48.

Galloway, A. (2013) Emergent media technologies, speculation, expectation, and human/nonhuman relations. *Journal of Broadcasting & Electronic Media*, 57 (1): 53–65.

Gerlitz, C. and Helmond, A. (2013) The like economy: Social buttons and the data-intensive web. *New Media & Society*, 15 (8): 1348–65.

Gerlitz, C. and Lury, C. (2014) Social media and self-evaluating assemblages: On numbers, orderings and values. *Distinktion: Scandinavian Journal of Social Theory*, 15 (2): 174–88.

Giddens, A. (1991) *Modernity and Self Identity*. Cambridge: Polity.

Gillespie, T. (2014) The relevance of algorithms. In T. Gillespie, P. J. Boczkowski, and K. A. Foot, eds, *Media Technologies: Essays on Communication, Materiality, and Society*, 167–93. Cambridge, MA: MIT Press.

Gillespie, T., Boczkowski, P. J., and Foot, K. A. (2014) Introduction. In T. Gillespie, P. J. Boczkowski, and K. A. Foot eds, *Media Technologies: Essays on Communication, Materiality, and Society*, 1–19. Cambridge, MA: MIT Press.

Gitelman, L. and Jackson, V. (2013) Introduction. In L. Gitelman, ed., *Raw Data Is an Oxymoron*, 1–14. Cambridge, MA: MIT Press.

Graham, C. (2014) Study: Wearable technology and preventive healthcare. TechnologyAdvice. http://technologyadvice.com/medical/blog/study-wearable-technology-preventative-healthcare (accessed 5 January 2015).

Greengard, S. (2015) *The Internet of Things*. Cambridge, MA: MIT Press.

Gregg, M. (2015) Inside the data spectacle. *Television & New Media*, 16 (1): 37–51.

Grosser, B. (2014) What do metrics want? How quantification prescribes social interaction on Facebook. *Computational Culture*, 9 November. http://computationalculture.net/article/what-do-metrics-want (accessed 16 November 2014).

Hacking, I. (1990) *The Taming of Chance*. Cambridge: Cambridge University Press.

Haggerty, K. and Ericson, R. (2000) The surveillant assemblage. *British Journal of Sociology*, 51 (4): 605–22.

Haraway, D. (1991) *Simians, Cyborgs and Women: The Reinvention of Nature*. London: Free Association.

Harsin, J. (2015) Regimes of posttruth, postpolitics, and attention economies. *Communication, Culture & Critique*, 8 (2): 327–33.

Hartmann, M. (2013) From domestication to mediated mobilism. *Mobile Media & Communication*, 1 (1): 42–9.

Hartzog, W. and Selinger, E. (2013) The chilling implications of democratizing big data: Facebook graph search is only the beginning. Forbes. http://www.forbes.com/sites/privacynotice/

2013/10/16/the-chilling-implications-of-democratizing-big
-data-facebook-graph-search-is-only-the-beginning (accessed 17
October 2013).

Hayles, N. K. (2008) *How We Became Posthuman: Virtual Bodies
in Cybernetics, Literature, and Informatics*. Chicago, IL: University of Chicago Press.

Hazleden, R. (2003) Love yourself: The relationship of the self with
itself in popular self-help texts. *Journal of Sociology*, 39 (4):
413–28.

Heath, A. (2015) Apple boss: We have a human right to privacy. *The Telegraph*, 27 February. http://www.telegraph.co.uk/
technology/apple/11441265/Terrorists-should-be-eliminated-says
-Apples-Tim-Cook.html (accessed 15 March 2015).

Heikkinen, M.-P. and Teivainen, A. (2014) Self-tracking trending
up in Finland. *Helsinki Times*, 21 June. http://www.helsinkitimes
.fi/lifestyle/10982-self-tracking-trending-up-in-finland.html
(accessed 5 July 2014).

Helmond, A. (2013) The algorithmization of the hyperlink. *Computational Culture*, 16 November. http://computationalculture
.net/article/the-algorithmization-of-the-hyperlink (accessed 12
November 2013).

Hesse, M. (2008) Bytes of life. *Washington Post*, 9 September.
http://www.washingtonpost.com/wp-dyn/content/article/2008/
09/08/AR2008090802681.html (accessed 28 August 2012).

Hon, D. (2012) Fitness by design. *Domus*. http://www.domusweb.it/
en/design/2012/11/28/fitness-by-design.html (accessed 20 March
2014).

Hon, D. (2014) Episode sixty two: Wearables unworn: Look at
what they want. *Extenuating Circumstances*, 18 April. http://
tinyletter.com/danhon/letters/episode-sixty-two-wearables
-unworn-look-at-what-they-want (accessed 9 June 2013).

Hui Kyong Chun, W. (2011) Crisis, crisis, crisis, or sovereignty and
networks. *Theory, Culture & Society*, 28 (6): 91–112.

Humer, C. and Finkle, J. (2014) Your medical record is worth
more to hackers than your credit card. Reuters US. http://
www.reuters.com/article/2014/09/24/us-cybersecurity-hospitals
-idUSKCN0HJ21I20140924 (accessed 26 July 2015).

IEEE (1997) *Digest of Papers of the First International Symposium on Wearable Computers*. http://ieeexplore.ieee.org/xpl/
mostRecentIssue.jsp?reload=true&punumber=4968 (accessed 12
January 2015).

Intel IT Center (2014) Digital empathy: Wearables and emotional IQ. Intel IT Peer Network. https://communities.intel.com/
community/itpeernetwork/blog/2014/09/09/digital-empathy
-wearables-and-emotional-iq (accessed 26 January 2015).

John, N. (2013) Sharing and Web 2.0: The emergence of a keyword. *New Media & Society*, 15 (2): 167–82.

Jordan, M. and Pfarr, N. (2014) The quantified us. Artefact Group. http://www.artefactgroup.com/content/the-quantified-us (accessed 17 March 2014).

Kaye, K. (2014) FTC: Fitness apps can help you shred calories – and privacy. Ad Age. http://adage.com/article/privacy-and-regulation/ftc-signals-focus-health-fitness-data-privacy/293080 (accessed 22 December 2014).

Keane, H. (2000) Setting yourself free: Techniques of recovery. *Health*, 4 (3): 324–46.

Kelly, K. (2007) What is the quantified self? Quantified Self. http://quantifiedself.com/2007/page/3 (accessed 27 June 2014).

Kelly, K. (2011) Self-tracking? You will. http://www.kk.org/thetechnium/archives/2011/03/self-tracking_y.php (accessed 12 August 2013).

Kelly, P. (2013) *The Self as Enterprise: Foucault and the Spirit of 21st Century Capitalism*. Farnham: Gower Publishing.

Khot, R., Hjorth, L., and Mueller, F. F. (2014) Understanding physical activity through 3D printed material artifacts. In *Proceedings of Conference on Human Factors in Computing Systems*, 3835–44. Toronto: ACM.

Khot, R., Lee, J., Munz, H., Aggarwal, D., and Mueller, F. (2014) TastyBeats: Making mocktails with heartbeats. In *Proceedings of Designing Interactive Futures*, 467–70. Vancouver: ACM.

Kitchin, R. (2014) *The Data Revolution: Big Data, Open Data, Data Infrastructures and Their Consequences*. London: Sage.

Kitchin, R. and Dodge, M. (2011) *Code/Space: Software and Everyday Life*. Cambridge, MA: MIT Press.

Kitchin, R. and Lauriault, T. (2014) Towards critical data studies: Charting and unpacking data assemblages and their work. Social Science Research Network. http://papers.ssrn.com/sol3/papers.cfm?abstract_id=2474112 (accessed 27 August 2014).

Lasch, C. (1991 [1979]) *The Culture of Narcissism: American Life in an Age of Diminishing Expectations*. New York: Norton.

Lash, S. (2006) Life (Vitalism). *Theory, Culture & Society*, 23 (2–3): 323–29.

Lash, S. (2007) Power after hegemony: Cultural studies in mutation? *Theory, Culture & Society*, 24 (3): 55–78.

Latour, B. (2005) *Reassembling the Social: An Introduction to Actor–Network Theory*. Oxford: Clarendon.

Law, J. and Hassard, J. (1999) *Actor–Network Theory and After*. Oxford: Blackwell Publishers.

Leder, D. (1990) *The Absent Body*. Chicago, IL: University of Chicago Press.

Ledger, D. and McCaffrey, D. (2014) *Inside Wearables: How the Science of Human Behavior Change Offers the Secret to Long-Term Engagement*. Endeavour Partners. http://endeavourpartners .net/assets/Wearables-and-the-Science-of-Human-Behavior -Change-EP4.pdf (accessed 9 September 2015)

Lee, J. and Kristensen, M. B. (2015) The best wearables will be the ones you throw away. Co.Design. http://www.fastcodesign.com/ 3044716/the-best-wearables-will-be-the-ones-you-throw-away (accessed 12 April 2015).

Lee, M. (2014) Apple still has plenty of your data for the Feds. The Intercept. https://firstlook.org/theintercept/2014/09/22/apple -data (accessed 15 March 2015).

Li, I., Dey, A., and Forlizzi, J. (2010) A stage-based model of personal informatics systems. In *Proceedings of the SIGCHI Conference on Human Factors in Computing Systems*, 557–66. Atlanta, GA: ACM.

Li, I., Dey, A. K., and Forlizzi, J. (2011) Understanding my data, myself: Supporting self-reflection with ubicomp technologies. In *Proceedings of the Thirteenth International Conference on Ubiquitous Computing*, 405–15. Beijing: ACM.

Libert, T. (2014) Health privacy online: Patients at risk. In S. Pena Gangadharan, V. Eubanks, and S. Barocas, eds., *Data and Discrimination: Collected Essays*, 11–15. Washington, DC: Open Technology Institute/New America Foundation.

LIX Index (2002) Welcome. http://www.lucykimbell.com/lix (accessed 18 September 2015).

LIX Index (2014) Welcome to the LIX Index: Introduction by Lucy Kimbell. http://lixindex.co.uk (accessed 20 June 2014).

LIX Index (2015) Reports. http://lixindex.co.uk/reports.html (accessed 11 April 2015).

Lloyd, A. (2014) In the loop: Designing conversations with algorithms. NYT Labs. http://blog.nytlabs.com/2014/04/07/in-the -loop-designing-conversations-with-algorithms (accessed 27 July 2014).

Longhurst, R. (2000) *Bodies: Exploring Fluid Boundaries*. London: Routledge.

Low, K. E. Y. (2013) Olfactive frames of remembering: Theorizing self, senses and society. *The Sociological Review*, 61 (4): 688–708.

Lupton, D. (1995a) The embodied computer/user. *Body & Society*, 1 (3–4): 97–112.

Lupton, D. (1995b) *The Imperative of Health: Public Health and the Regulated Body*. London: Sage.

Lupton, D. (2012) *Medicine as Culture: Illness, Disease and the Body*, 3rd edn. London: Sage.

Lupton, D. (2013a) The digitally engaged patient: Self-monitoring and self-care in the digital health era. *Social Theory and Health*, 11 (3): 256–70.

Lupton, D. (2013b) *Fat*. London: Routledge.

Lupton, D. (2014) The commodification of patient opinion: The digital patient experience economy in the age of big data. *Sociology of Health & Illness*, 36 (6): 856–69.

Lupton, D. (2015a) *Digital Sociology*. London: Routledge.

Lupton, D. (2015b) Health promotion in the digital era: A critical commentary. *Health Promotion International*, 30 (1): 174–83.

Lupton, D. (2015c) Quantified sex: A critical analysis of sexual and reproductive self-tracking using apps. *Culture, Health & Sexuality*, 17 (4): 440–53.

Lury, C. (1997) *Prosthetic Culture: Photography, Memory and Identity*. London: Routledge.

Lyon, D. (2002) Everyday surveillance: Personal data and social classifications. *Information, Communication & Society*, 5 (2): 242–57.

Lyon, D. (2007) *Surveillance Studies: An Overview*. Cambridge: Polity.

Lyon, D. (2010) Surveillance, power and everyday life. In P. Kalantzis-Cope and K. Gherab-Martin, eds, *Emerging Digital Spaces in Contemporary Society*, 107–20. Basingstoke: Palgrave Macmillan.

Lyon, D. and Bauman, Z. (2013) *Liquid Surveillance: A Conversation*. Oxford: Wiley Blackwell.

Mackenzie, A. (2005) The performativity of code: Software and cultures of circulation. *Theory, Culture & Society*, 22 (1): 71–92.

Mann, S. (1997) An historical account of the 'WearComp' and 'WearCam' inventions developed for applications in 'personal imaging'. In *Digest of Papers of the First International Symposium on Wearable Computers*, 66–73. Cambridge, MA: IEEE Computer Society.

Mann, S. (2013) Steve Mann: My 'augmediated' life. IEEE Spectrum. http://spectrum.ieee.org/geek-life/profiles/steve-mann-my-augmediated-life (accessed 22 February 2015).

Mann, S. and Ferenbok, J. (2013) New media and the power politics of sousveillance in a surveillance-dominated world. *Surveillance & Society*, 11 (1/2): 18–34.

Manovich, L. (2013) *Software Takes Command*. London: Bloomsbury.

Marcus, G. (2006) Assemblage. *Theory, Culture & Society*, 23 (2/3): 101–6.

McClusky, M. (2009) The Nike experiment: How the shoe giant unleashed the power of personal metrics. *Wired*. http://archive.wired.com/medtech/health/magazine/17-07/lbnp_nike?currentPage=all (accessed 3 September 2014).

McCosker, A. and Wilken, R. (2014) Rethinking 'big data' as visual knowledge: The sublime and the diagrammatic in data visualisation. *Visual Studies*, 29 (2): 155–64.

Metz, R. (2014) My life, logged. *MIT Technology Review*. http://www.technologyreview.com/review/528076/my-life-logged (accessed 13 June 2014).

Meyer, E. (2014) Inadvertent algorithmic cruelty. Meyerweb.com. http://meyerweb.com/eric/thoughts/2014/12/24/inadvertent-algorithmic-cruelty (accessed 11 March 2015).

Millsaps, B. B. (2014) SweetHearts offers printed chocolates as reward in new diet and exercise concept. 3D Print.com. http://3dprint.com/21241/sweethearts-chocolate-reward (accessed 1 April 2015).

MIT Media Lab Playful Systems (2014) 20 day stranger. The Dalai Lama Center for Ethics and Transformative Values at MIT. http://www.20daystranger.com (accessed 9 June 2014).

Mod, C. (2012) Paris and the data mind. The Morning News. http://www.themorningnews.org/article/paris-and-the-data-mind (accessed 21 April 2015).

Montini, L. (2013) Susannah Fox Q&A on Pew's latest health tracking report. Health 2.0 News. http://www.health2con.com/news/2013/01/30/susannah-fox-tracking (accessed 20 August 2014).

Morozov, E. (2013) *To Save Everything, Click Here: Technology, Solutionism and the Urge to Fix Problems That Don't Exist*. London: Allen Lane.

Morris (2014) Narrative camera: Morris. https://mokestrel.wordpress.com/2014/10/30/narrative-camera (accessed 2 November 2014).

MyLifeBits (2015) MyLifeBits. http://research.microsoft.com/en-us/projects/mylifebits (accessed 5 January 2015).

Nafus, D. (2014) Stuck data, dead data, and disloyal data: The stops and starts in making numbers into social practices. *Distinktion: Scandinavian Journal of Social Theory*, 15 (2): 208–22.

Nafus, D. and Sherman, J. (2014) This one does not go up to 11: The Quantified Self movement as an alternative big data practice. *International Journal of Communication*, 8: 1785–94.

NAIC (2014) Usage-based insurance and telematics. National Association of Insurance Commissioners and the Center for Insurance Policy and Research. http://www.naic.org/cipr_topics/topic_usage_based_insurance.htm (accessed 2 August 2014).

Neyland, D. (2015) On organizing algorithms. *Theory, Culture & Society*, 32 (1): 119–32.

Nielsen, C. (2014a) Hacking health: How consumers use smartphones and wearable tech to track their health. http://www.nielsen.com/us/en/insights/news/2014/hacking-health-how-consumers-use-smartphones-and-wearable-tech-to-track-their-health.html (accessed 10 May 2014).

Nielsen, C. (2014b) Tech-styles: Are consumers really interested in wearing tech on their sleeves? http://www.nielsen.com/us/en/insights/news/2014/tech-styles-are-consumers-really-interested-in-wearing-tech-on-their-sleeves.html (accessed 10 May 2014).

Nissenbaum, H. (2011) A contextual approach to privacy online. *Daedalus*, 140 (4): 32–48.

Nuffield Council on Bioethics (2015) *The Collection, Linking and Use of Data in Biomedical Research and Health Care: Ethical Issues*. http://nuffieldbioethics.org/wp-content/uploads/Biological_and_health_data_web.pdf (accessed 24 September 2015).

Oh, J. and Lee, U. (2015) Exploring UX issues in quantified self technologies. In *Proceedings of the Eighth International Conference on Mobile Computing and Ubiquitous Networking*, 53–9. Hakodate, Japan: IEEE.

Olson, P. (2014a) Fitbit data now being used in the courtroom. Forbes. http://www.forbes.com/sites/parmyolson/2014/11/16/fitbit-data-court-room-personal-injury-claim (accessed 16 November 2014).

Olson, P. (2014b) Get ready for wearable tech to plug into health insurance. Forbes. http://www.forbes.com/sites/parmyolson/2014/06/19/wearable-tech-health-insurance (accessed 21 June 2014).

Olwyn, G. (2015) Compulsory quantified self. Your Eatopia. http://www.youreatopia.com/blog/2015/1/27/compulsory-quantified-self.html (accessed 1 February 2015).

Open Humans (2015) About us. https://www.openhumans.org/about/#project (accessed 7 April 2015).

Open Lab (formerly Digital Interaction at Culture Lab) (2011) Wearable acoustic monitor. http://di.ncl.ac.uk/things/wam (accessed 7 February 2015).

Oxford Dictionaries (2015) Self-tracking. http://www.oxforddictionaries.com/definition/english/self-tracking (accessed 28 April 2015).

Pantzar, M. and Ruckenstein, M. (2015) The heart of everyday analytics: Emotional, material and practical extensions in self-tracking market. *Consumption Markets & Culture*, 18 (1): 92–109.

Parrish, A. (2012) Gamification keeps me going (aka I'm the self-tracking type). Bikestyle. http://bikestylespokane.com/2012/06/

09/gamification-keeps-me-going-aka-im-the-self-tracking-type
-an-andrea-post (accessed 28 June 2014).

Pasquale, F. (2014) The dark market for personal data. *The New York Times*, 16 October. http://www.nytimes.com/2014/10/17/opinion/the-dark-market-for-personal-data.html (accessed 8 April 2015).

Pasquale, F. (2015) The algorithmic self. *The Hedgework Review*, 17 (1). http://www.iasc-culture.org/THR/THR_article_2015_Spring_Pasquale.php (accessed 15 March 2015).

Paz, C. (2013) 'Small, n=me, data': Deborah Estrin visits the GovLab. GovLab. http://thegovlab.org/deborah-estrin-visits-the-govlab (accessed 30 July 2014).

Peake, B. (2015) Decolonizing design anthropology with Tinn. Blog.CASTAC.Org. http://blog.castac.org/2015/04/designing-tinn (accessed 23 April 2015).

Personal Informatics (2015) Tools. http://www.personalinformatics.org/tools (accessed 18 April 2015).

Peters, A. (2015) Don't relax: Uncomfortability is the new convenience. FastCompany. http://www.fastcoexist.com/3040839/world-changing-ideas/dont-relax-uncomfortability-is-the-new-convenience?imm_mid=0cf6ee&cmp=em-iot-na-na-newsltr_iot_20150402 (accessed 12 April 2015).

Petersen, A. and Lupton, D. (1996) *The New Public Health: Health and Self in the Age of Risk*. London: Sage.

Pettypiece, S. (2014) Sexually active? How much do you drink? Your workplace health records may not be as private as you think. Bloomberg. http://www.bloomberg.com/news/2014–12–16/your-wellness-program-at-work-may-not-be-as-private-as-you-think.html (accessed 20 December 2014).

Pettypiece, S. and Robertson, J. (2014) Hospitals are mining patients' credit card data to predict who will get sick. Bloomberg. http://www.bloomberg.com/bw/articles/2014–07–03/hospitals-are-mining-patients-credit-card-data-to-predict-who-will-get-sick (accessed 8 April 2015).

Pew Research Center (2014) *Public Perceptions of Privacy and Security in the post-Snowden Era*. Pew Research Internet Project. http://www.pewinternet.org/2014/11/12/public-privacy-perceptions/# (accessed 20 November 2014).

Picard, R. (2000) *Affective Computing*. Cambridge, MA: MIT Press.

Pink, S. (2009) *Doing Sensory Ethnography*. London: Sage.

Pink, S. and Leder Mackley, K. (2013) Saturated and situated: Expanding the meaning of media in the routines of everyday life. *Media, Culture & Society*, 35 (6): 677–91.

Pink, S. and Leder Mackley, K. (2014) Moving, making and atmosphere: Routines of home as sites for mundane improvisation. *Mobilities*, 4: 1–17. doi: 10.1080/17450101.2014.957066.

Polonetsky, J. and Tene, O. (2013) Privacy and big data: Making ends meet. *Stanford Law Review Online*, 65. http://www .stanfordlawreview.org/online/privacy-and-big-data/privacy-and -big-data (accessed 4 September 2013).

Poynter, R. (2014) A big picture of the trends in mobile market research. GreenBook. http://www.greenbookblog.org/2014/07/ 30/a-big-picture-of-the-trends-in-mobile-market-research/?utm _content=buffer209de&utm_medium=social&utm_source =linkedin.com&utm_campaign=buffer (accessed 2 August 2014).

Predict (2015) Towards a Magna Carta for big data: Social and ethical challenges and opportunities for big data. Data Ethics Workshop, Insight Ireland Centre for Data Analytics. http://predictconference.com/workshops/ethics-workshop.html (accessed 23 September 2015).

Purpura, S., Schwanda, V., Williams, K., Stubler, W., and Sengers, P. (2011) Fit4life: The design of a persuasive technology promoting healthy behavior and ideal weight. In *Proceedings of the SIGCHI Conference on Human Factors in Computing Systems*, 423–32. Vancouver: ACM.

Quantified Self (2015a) About the Quantified Self. http:// quantifiedself.com/about (accessed 16 April 2015).

Quantified Self (2015b) Guide to self-tracking tools. http:// quantifiedself.com/guide/tools?sort=reviews&pg=1 (accessed 18 April 2015).

Quantified Self (2015c) Quantified self: Self-knowledge through numbers. Home page. http://quantifiedself.com (accessed 5 February 2015).

Quantified Self (2015d) Wikipedia article. http://en.wikipedia.org/ wiki/Quantified_Self (accessed 28 April 2015).

Quantified self meetup groups (2015) Quantified self meetups. http://quantified-self.meetup.com (accessed 25 July 2015).

The quantified self: Data gone wild? (2013) PBS Newshour. http:// www.pbs.org/newshour/bb/science/july-dec13/quantifiedself_09 –28.html (accessed 13 October 2013).

Raley, R. (2013) Dataveillance and countervailance. In L. Gitelman, ed., *'Raw Data' Is an Oxymoron*, 121–45. Cambridge, MA: MIT Press.

Ramirez, E. (2013) How can we get more meaning out of our data? http://quantifiedself.com/2013/08/how-can-we-get-more -meaning-out-of-our-data (accessed 12 August 2013).

Ramirez, E. (2014) Tidings: QS St. Louis show & tell. Quantified Self. http://quantifiedself.com/2014/07/tidings-st-louis-showtell (accessed 29 July 2014).

Ramirez, E. (2015) Communities, climate, environment, and health. Quantified Self. http://quantifiedself.com/2015/04/communities -climate-environment-and-health (accessed 18 April 2015).

Ratto, M., Wylie, S. A., and Jalbert, K. (2014) Introduction to the special forum on critical making as research program. *The Information Society*, 30 (2): 85–95.

Regalado, A. (2013) Stephen Wolfram on personal analytics. *MIT Technology Review*. http://www.technologyreview.com/ news/514356/stephen-wolfram-on-personal-analytics (accessed 14 June 2014).

RescueTime (2014) Home. https://www.rescuetime.com (accessed 22 June 2014).

Rey, P. J. (2012) Alienation, exploitation, and social media. *American Behavioral Scientist*, 56 (4): 399–420.

Rich, E. and Miah, A. (2009) Prosthetic surveillance: The medical governance of health bodies in cyberspace. *Surveillance & Society*, 6 (2): 163–77.

Ritzer, G. (2014) Prosumption: Evolution, revolution, or eternal return of the same? *Journal of Consumer Culture*, 14 (1): 3–24.

Roberts, S. (2012) Quantified self utopia: What would it look like? Quantified Self. http://quantifiedself.com/2012/10/quantified-self -utopia-what-would-it-look-like (accessed 12 March 2015).

Robinson, D., Yu, H., and Rieke, A. (2014) *Civil Rights, Big Data, and Our Algorithmic Future: A September 2014 Report on Social Justice and Technology*. Robinson + Yu. https://bigdata.fairness .io/wp-content/uploads/2014/11/Civil_Rights_Big_Data_and _Our_Algorithmic-Future_v1.1.pdf (accessed 19 September 2015).

Rogers, R. (2013) *Digital Methods*. Cambridge, MA: MIT Press.

Rooksby, J., Rost, M., Morrison, A., and Chalmers, M. C. (2014) Personal tracking as lived informatics. In *Proceedings of the Thirty-second Annual ACM Conference on Human Factors in Computing Systems*, 1163–72. Toronto: ACM.

Rose, N. (1990) *Governing the Soul: The Shaping of the Private Self*. London: Routledge.

Rose, N. (1996) *Inventing Our Selves: Psychology, Power and Personhood*. Cambridge: Cambridge University Press.

Rose, N. (2007) *The Politics of Life Itself: Biomedicine, Power, and Subjectivity in the Twenty-First Century*. Princeton, NJ: Princeton University Press.

Rose, N. (2008) The value of life: Somatic ethics and the spirit of biocapital. *Daedalus*, 137 (1): 36–48.

Rosen, J. (2012) The right to be forgotten. *Stanford Law Review Online*, 64 (88). http://www.stanfordlawreview.org/online/privacy-paradox/right-to-be-forgotten (accessed 21 November 2013).

Rosenblat, A., Kneese, T., and boyd, d. (2014) Networked employment discrimination. Data & Society Research Institute Working Paper. http://www.datasociety.net/pubs/fow/EmploymentDiscrimination.pdf (accessed 11 October 2014).

Rosenblat, A., Wikelius, K., boyd, d., Pena Gangadharan, S., and Yu, C. (2014) *Data and Civil Rights: Health Primer*. Data & Society Research Institute. http://www.datacivilrights.org/pubs/2014–1030/Health.pdf (accessed 16 December 2014).

Rosenzweig, P. (2012) Whither privacy? *Surveillance & Society*, 10 (3/4): 344–7.

Ruckenstein, M. (2014) Visualized and interacted life: Personal analytics and engagements with data doubles. *Societies*, 4 (1): 68–84.

Ruppert, E. (2011) Population objects: Interpassive subjects. *Sociology*, 45 (2): 218–33.

Ryan, S. E. (2014) *Garments of Paradise: Wearable Discourse in the Digital Age*. Cambridge, MA: MIT Press.

Sarasohn-Kahn, J. (2014) *Here's Looking at You: How Personal Health Information Is Being Tracked and Used*. California Healthcare Foundation. http://www.chcf.org/~/media/MEDIA%20LIBRARY%20Files/PDF/PDF%20H/PDF%20HeresLookingPersonalHealthInfo.pdf (accessed 24 September 2015).

Savage, M. (2013) The 'social life of methods': A critical introduction. *Theory, Culture & Society*, 30 (4): 3–21.

Sellar, S. (2014) A feel for numbers: Affect, data and education policy. *Critical Studies in Education*, 56 (1): 131–46.

Sellen, A. J. and Whittaker, S. (2010) Beyond total capture: A constructive critique of lifelogging. *Communications of the ACM*, 53 (5): 70–7.

Shilling, C. (1993) *The Body and Society*. London: Sage.

Singer, N. (2015) With a few bits of data, researchers identify 'anonymous' people. *The New York Times*, 29 January. http://mobile.nytimes.com/blogs/bits/2015/01/29/with-a-few-bits-of-data-researchers-identify-anonymous-people/?_r=0&referrer = (accessed 8 April 2015).

Small Data Lab (2014) You + your data: The Building Blocks of Small Data Apps. smalldata.io (accessed 23 September 2015).

Snow, S., Buys, L., Roe, P., and Brereton, M. (2013) Curiosity to cupboard: Self reported disengagement with energy use feedback over time. In *Proceedings of the Twenty-fifth Australian*

Computer-Human Interaction Conference: Augmentation, Application, Innovation, Collaboration, 245–54. Adelaide: ACM.

Strava (2015) About us. http://www.strava.com/about (accessed 26 January 2015).

Stusak, S., Tabard, A., Sauka, F., Khot, R. A., and Butz, A. (2014) Activity sculptures: Exploring the impact of physical visualizations on running activity. *IEEE Transactions on Visualization and Computer Graphics*, 20 (12): 2201–10.

Swan, M. (2012a) Health 2050: The realization of personalized medicine through crowdsourcing, the quantified self, and the participatory biocitizen. *Journal of Personalized Medicine*, 2 (3): 93–118.

Swan, M. (2012b) Sensor mania! The Internet of Things, wearable computing, objective metrics, and the Quantified Self 2.0. *Journal of Sensor and Actuator Networks*, 1 (3): 217–53.

Swan, M. (2013) The quantified self: Fundamental disruption in big data science and biological discovery. *Big Data*, 1 (2). http://online.liebertpub.com/doi/abs/10.1089/big.2012.0002 (accessed 2 March 2014).

Tanner, C., Maher, J., and Fraser, S. (2013) *Vanity: 21st Century Selves*. Basingstoke: Palgrave Macmillan.

Tene, O. and Polonetsky, J. (2013) A theory of creepy: Technology, privacy and shifting social norms. *Yale Journal of Law & Technology*, 16: 59–134.

Thaler, R. and Sustein, C. (2009) *Nudge: Improving Decisions about Health, Wealth, and Happiness*. New York: Penguin Books.

Thompson, C. (2006) A head for detail. FastCompany. http://www.fastcompany.com/58044/head-detail (accessed 6 February 2015).

Thrift, N. (2005) *Knowing Capitalism*. London: Sage.

Thrift, N. (2014) The 'sentient' city and what it may portend. *Big Data & Society*, 1 (1). http://bds.sagepub.com/content/1/1/2053951714532241.full.pdf+html (accessed 1 April 2014).

Till, C. (2014) Exercise as labour: Quantified self and the transformation of exercise into labour. *Societies*, 4 (3): 446–62.

Topol, E. (2015) *The Patient Will See You Now: The Future of Medicine Is in Your Hands*. New York: Basic Books.

Torgan, C. (2012) A shiny new activity tracker: Technology as talisman? *Kinetics*. http://caroltorgan.com/shine-activity-tracker (accessed 25 January 2015).

Totaro, P. and Ninno, D. (2014) The concept of algorithm as an interpretative key of modern rationality. *Theory, Culture & Society*, 31 (4): 29–49.

Trinity College Dublin Science Gallery (2015) Grow your own life: Life after nature. https://dublin.sciencegallery.com/growyourown (accessed 20 March 2015).

Turkle, S. (2007) Introduction: The things that matter. In S. Turkle, ed., *Evocative Objects: Things We Think With*, 3–10. Cambridge, MA: MIT Press.

Turney, J. (2015) How to design the future, *Aeon*. http://aeon .co/magazine/technology/how-design-fiction-imagines-future -technology (accessed 20 March 2015).

van der Ploeg, I. (1999) The illegal body: 'Eurodac' and the politics of biometric identification. *Ethics and Information Technology*, 1 (4): 295–302.

van der Ploeg, I. (2003) Biometrics and privacy: A note on the politics of theorizing technology. *Information, Communication & Society*, 6 (1): 85–104.

van Dijck, J. (2013) *The Culture of Connectivity: A Critical History of Social Media*. Oxford: Oxford University Press.

van Dijck, J. (2014) Datafication, dataism and dataveillance: Big data between scientific paradigm and ideology. *Surveillance & Society*, 12 (2): 197–208.

van Mamen, M. (2010) The pedagogy of Momus technologies: Facebook, privacy and online intimacy. *Qualitative Health Research*, 20 (8): 1023–32.

Virgin Pulse (2015) Technology to replenish the modern worker. http://www.virginpulse.com/our-products (accessed 12 April 2015).

Waldby, C. (1997) The body and the digital archive: The Visible Human Project and the computerization of medicine. *Health*, 1 (2): 227–43.

Walgreens (2014) Walgreens rewards healthy activities through first community pharmacy program to include behavior change training based on Dr BJ Fogg's methodology. Walgreens. http://news.walgreens.com/article_display.cfm?article_id=5883 (accessed 3 August 2014).

Wellcome Trust (2013) *Summary Report of Qualitative Research into Public Attitudes to Personal Data and Linking Personal Data*. The Wellcome Trust. http://www.wellcome.ac.uk/stellent/ groups/corporatesite/@msh_grants/documents/web_document/ wtp053205.pdf (accessed 12 September 2015).

Werbin, K. (2011) Spookipedia: Intelligence, social media and biopolitics. *Media, Culture & Society*, 33 (8): 1254–65.

Whitson, J. (2013) Gaming the quantified self. *Surveillance & Society*, 11 (1/2): 163–76.

Williams, K. (2013) The weight of things lost: Self-knowledge and personal informatics. Personal Informatics. http://www

.personalinformatics.org/docs/chi2013/williams.pdf (accessed 12 May 2014).

Wolf, G. (2009) Know thyself: Tracking every facet of life, from sleep to mood to pain, 24/7/365. *Wired*. http://archive.wired.com/medtech/health/magazine/17–07/lbnp_knowthyself (accessed 12 October 2013).

Wolf, G. (2010) The data-driven life. *The New York Times*, 28 April. http://www.nytimes.com/2010/05/02/magazine/02self-measurement-t.html?pagewanted=all&_r=0 (accessed 22 February 2013).

Wolf, G. (2013) Photo-life-logging experiment at the QS conference. Quantified Self. https://forum.quantifiedself.com/thread-photo-life-logging-experiment-at-the-qs-conference (accessed 11 September 2014).

Wolf, G. (2014) Access matters. Quantified Self. http://quantifiedself.com/page/5 (accessed 4 September 2014).

XOX Emotional Technology Platform (2014) Website. http://xoxemotionaltech.com (accessed 31 July 2014).

Zamosky, L. (2014) Digital health tools are a growing part of workplace wellness programs. iHealthBeat. http://www.ihealthbeat.org/insight/2014/digital-health-tools-are-a-growing-part-of-workplace-wellness-programs (accessed 2 August 2014).

Index